JAPANESE WOODWORKING TOOLS

. . .

JAPANESE WOODWORKING TOOLS

Selection, Care & Use

■ ■ ■

Henry Lanz

Sterling Publishing Co., Inc.   New York

Edited by Michael Cea

Library of Congress Cataloging in Publication Data
Lanz, Henry.
 Japanese woodworking tools.

 Bibliography: p.
 Includes index.
 1. Woodworking tools—Japan. I. Title.
TT186.L36 1985   684´.082´0952   85-9989
ISBN 0-8069-6236-4 (pbk.)

Second Printing, 1985

Copyright © 1985 by Henry Lanz
Published by Sterling Publishing Co., Inc.
Two Park Avenue, New York, N.Y. 10016
Distributed in Australia by Capricorn Book Co. Pty. Ltd.
Unit 5C1 Lincoln St., Lane Cove, N.S.W. 2066
Distributed in the United Kingdom by Blandford Press
Link House, West Street, Poole, Dorset BH15 1LL, England
Distributed in Canada by Oak Tree Press Ltd.
‰ Canadian Manda Group, P.O. Box 920, Station U
Toronto, Ontario, Canada M8Z 5P9
Manufactured in the United States of America
All rights reserved

Acknowledgments

A list of sources for information used in writing this book would be almost endless. The toolmakers of Europe and Japan who have allowed me to inspect their operations and question their methods have been of invaluable assistance. In Japan I can cite Iyoroi, Uozumi, Nagaoke and Nanba. At Oak Village in Makigahora, a small village in the mountains of central Japan, a young commune of workers producing individual pieces of oak furniture by traditional methods gave freely of their time.

Mr. Tanaka of Miki and Mr. Muramatsu of Sanjo have spent many days shepherding me about their respective towns to meet various local toolmakers. In both of these towns, the local chambers of commerce have been most helpful. In Kobe, I had the privilege of a guided tour of the Takenaka Carpentry Tools Museum by its director during its opening week in July 1984.

A special acknowledgment goes to Toshio Ōdate, who provided me with my first intelligent introduction to Japanese tools. Over the years we have had many spirited discussions on the use and marketing of Japanese tools in the American marketplace. For anyone wanting the viewpoint of a craftsman who has learned his skills through the rigors of a Japanese apprenticeship, I recommend his book, *Japanese Woodworking Tools: Their Tradition, Spirit and Use* without reservation.

The tools shown have come either from the personal collections of Harry Troutman and myself or were furnished by the Garrett Wade Company of New York City. Harry Troutman has taken all the photographs used in this book. He is a business associate with a love of tools, not a professional photographer, and had to sacrifice a great deal of his own time. I thank his wife, Laura, for permitting their home to be used as a photography studio, and ask her forgiveness for the amazing number of hours that this project required.

Foreword

This book has two purposes. It is intended primarily to provide the craftsman who does not have first-hand experience with traditional Japanese tools with a practical introduction to their selection and use. It will also provide basic information on how they are made and how this affects their performance.

Since Japanese tools ultimately perform the same function as Western tools, there are many similarities. However, there are also some important differences. Japanese saws and planes cut on the pull stroke, while Western saws and planes cut on the push stroke. Japanese tools have cutting edges that are harder. Also, Japanese sharpening stones tend to cut faster for a given grit size.

It is very easy to make the transition to certain Japanese tools, but quite difficult, especially for the occasional user, to become adept with others when he is accustomed to the feel and action of Western tools. In certain instances, if the tools traditionally designed for the Japanese craftsman are modified they will perform better in the working conditions usually found in the Western workplace.

There are differences in the working conditions of Japanese and Western woodworkers. In the West, there is a greater use of hardwoods and far more variable climatic conditions. Also, more recreational woodworkers are engaged in demanding home projects.

The beginner will be able to pick up most modified Japanese tools (for example, saws and chisels) and use them without damaging them. Gradually, he will gain enough experience and confidence to pick and choose from the many varieties and qualities of Japanese tools currently appearing in the marketplace.

Table of Contents

Fig. 1. Japanese carpenters at work (wood block print, circa 1870). This print is one in a series depicting the construction of a house. Other prints from this series appear on pages 14 and 140.

Introduction

Japanese woodworking tools have only started gaining rapid acceptance in the United States within the past decade. On first glance they appear radically different from comparable tools used by the American craftsman. However, if one goes back into the 19th century and compares American, European and Japanese tools, many similarities begin to appear. For example, hundreds of American, European and Japanese special-purpose planes had their bodies formed from a piece of native hardwood. Generally, the better plane and chisel blades were hand-forged by the local blacksmith from iron with a welded steel insert for the cutting edge. Also, chisel handles were made of wood and sharpening was done with natural stones.

Before the end of the century, however, Great Britain and the United States, the two countries with the largest markets and the most advanced metalworking industries, had turned to mass-production techniques to fill the market demand for hand tools. This meant cast-iron plane bodies, drop-forged chisels and saw blades cut from rolled sheet steel. Meanwhile, in Europe and Japan, where national markets were smaller, the wood-bodied plane has remained even to this day the preferred quality plane.

The introduction of mass production effectively eliminated the small-toolmakers. While small, family tool firms still coexist with Stanley, Record, etc., in Europe, it is only in Japan that the cottage-tool industry has remained a significant market factor. As a result, the Japanese tool market has some of the characteristics of the English and American markets of the early twentieth century.

In Japan, the traditional plane body is still made from a single piece of wood. The absence of extreme variations in humidity and artificial heat in the workshop minimize the natural movement of the wood. In Europe, plane bodies are made of laminated pieces to reduce the effect of the different climate changes.

The Japanese plane blade is tapered and will seat itself when forced into a corresponding wedge-shaped slot. The European plane blade is flat and is fixed into position by forcing a tapered wooden wedge into the blade slot. Both methods compensate for wear in the slot: the wooden wedge goes down further into the slot; the tapered blade when ground back during sharpening becomes thicker.

In Europe, the popular saw for general woodworking is the frame saw (large bow saw). Here a wooden frame holds a comparatively thin saw blade in tension. In Japan, a thin blade is used in tension by cutting on the pull stroke. Both result in a thinner kerf then the English or American panel saw, which cuts on the push stroke. To do this, the blade must be thicker and the teeth set wider to reduce the natural tendency for the blade to bend when it binds in the kerf. The thinner blades require less force as they remove less wood during a cutting stroke. They also require more skill to use properly.

The mass-produced tools of America and England require less maintenance for everyday use. The steel plane is dimensionally stable as humidity varies. But it does not possess the more precise, although demanding, adjustment procedures required by the traditional Japanese and European wooden planes. This may be due in part to the fact that rigorous apprentice programs existed in these areas until recently. As technical skills have decreased, changes in tool design have appeared: blade-adjusting mechanisms on wooden planes in Germany; laminated planes; disposable saw blades; and, in Japan, chisel and plane blades without the hollow-ground back. These, as well as other refinements, make it easier for the beginning craftsman to make use of these conceptually different tools.

This book attempts to provide an introduction to the use of the basic traditional woodworking tools of Japan that are now available in the marketplace. Some of these tools will make certain jobs faster and easier than comparable Western tools, and most will provide an alternate and perhaps more aesthetically pleasing route to the desired end product. Usually, the same results can be accomplished whether good-quality American-, European- or Japanese-style tools are used.

In describing Japanese tools, I will try as much as possible to use Western terminology. It is usually not necessary to use Japanese terminology to describe Japanese tools. When an item is unique in concept to Japan, then the Japanese name will be used. For example, the two-sided combination rip/crosscut saw has no Western counterpart, and so is referred to by its Japanese name, *ryoba.* Conversely, a firmer or butt chisel will not be referred to in the text as an *atsu-nomi* or an *oire-nomi.* Appendix C (page 154) will help clarify these terms.

The text and illustrations will provide sufficient instructions for someone without experience to use Japanese tools along with Western tools. The book is not intended to be a manual on Japanese joinery. Emphasis will be placed on the use of tools for everyday requirements and not on the ultimate tool that can be produced by the master blacksmith and which commands a very high price. While this tool may be a joy to behold and use, most of us are by necessity going to buy and use those moderately priced tools that can produce the work we are capable of doing.

The opinions expressed in this book are drawn from more than fifty years of observation, study and experience. My first experiences with tools came when I was a young farm boy; I even had the chance to watch the town blacksmith at his work. Later I worked as a development engineer in the aerospace industry, and then in the United States, Europe and Japan in a variety of capacities such as an engineer, consultant or tool buyer. I have seen dirt-floored plants in northern England, hand-forging operations in southern Austria, and many other small and large, modern and outmoded, tool producers in the countries between. In Japan, I have met many of the toolmakers of Miki and Sanjo, as well as carpenters, cabinetmakers, carvers and turners in other sections of the country.

Fig. 2. Sharpening a large ripsaw (maebiki). *This figure is an ivory netsuke 1¼" (31.8 mm) high, signed* Hinoyojin.

I · SAWS

Of all the Japanese edge tools introduced to the Western woodworker, the saw has been the most popular. Its thin, very hard blade which cuts on the pull stroke is an efficient, fast-cutting tool. To use this type of saw properly requires very little change in work habits.

Since the time of the earliest known use of saws in Japan, they have been designed to cut on the pull stroke. There is no conclusive reason for this. Some experts point to the seated posture of the workman, while others cite the widespread use of soft, straight-grained cedar and cypress as the prime building materials. Others attest to the inherent accuracy of the pull saw. In contrast, saws used in China and Korea were designed to cut on the push stroke.

The only Western-style saw found in former times in Japanese woodworking is the large frame saw that was introduced from China about the 15th century. Its primary use was for the resawing of lumber. It was later replaced by wide-blade rip saws; as a result, the frame saw is little known in Japan today. The wood-block print on page 14 shows a resawing operation.

Since the Japanese saw blade is designed to cut on the pull stroke, it can be very thin, as there is no tendency for the blade to bend when used properly. This principle can be demonstrated by taking a ribbon or strip of paper, holding one end in each hand and pulling the strip taut, at which point it is a straight line. Conversely, when the ends are pushed together, the strip simply bends.

For the Western saw to remain straight on the push or power stroke, it must be stiffened by making it thicker. Even this additional thickness will not prevent the saw from bending if it catches or binds when cutting. If pushed too hard at the moment it snags, the saw will kink and a permanent crease may be set into the blade. To reduce this type of failure in the steel the blade must have a degree of ductility, which, by necessity, reduces its hardness. To compensate for this, some saws will have only the very tips of the teeth hardened.

Fig. 3. Japanese carpenters resawing timbers for house construction (wood block print, circa 1870).

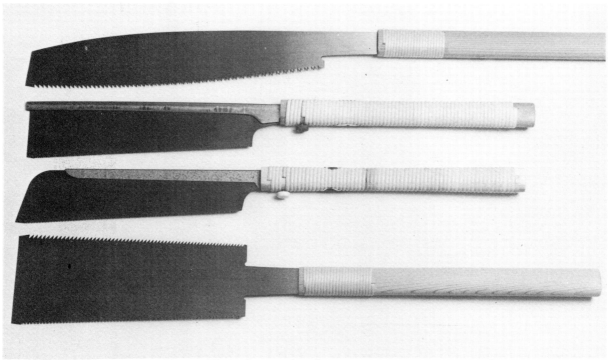

Fig. 4. Typical examples of carpenter's saws. From top to bottom: roughing saw, hardwood backsaw, softwood backsaw, and combination rip and crosscut saw.

If a Japanese saw binds on the pull or power stroke, there is no force to cause it to bend; therefore, it can be made considerably harder than its Western counterpart. This means that the blade is more brittle and a tooth will occasionally break off. This is not a disaster, and has little effect on the performance of the saw. However, if this blade is forced back through the cut on the return stroke and binds, it might even shatter. While the very best Western saw will have a hardness of $R_c 50$ (see the Glossary for a definition of Rockwell hardness), the better quality Japanese saw will have a hardness of $R_c 54$. If the teeth on a Japanese saw deform by bending instead of breaking off, it was probably an inferior-grade saw made of low-grade steel for a child.

One thing that is immediately noticeable in using a saw with a thinner blade and minimal set, and consequently narrower kerf, is that it cuts faster and with less effort. This re-

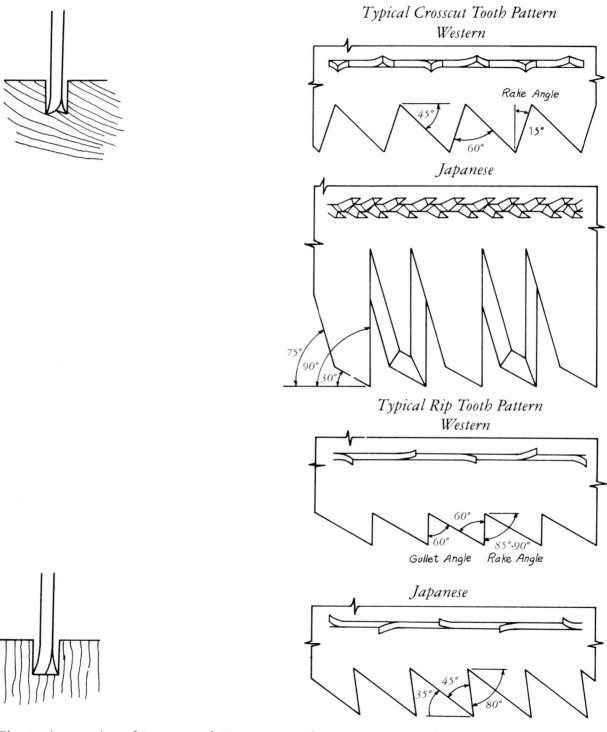

Fig. 5. A comparison of Japanese and Western saw teeth patterns (courtesy of Garrett Wade Company).

sults from removing less wood for a given cut. This same result can be obtained with a frame saw, which uses a long thin blade held in tension. While its tensioned blade cannot buckle, the encompassing frame can make it awkward to use.

There remain only a few artisans in Japan who can make a saw entirely by hand. This process includes hand-forging a laminated blade, tempering and tensioning, scraping, filing and setting the teeth. Most saws made today will at least start from a coil of factory-made steel strip and be furnace heat-treated. Then they will be machine ground and tensioned, the teeth cut and then machine set. This is no different from a Western saw, and when properly made the tool will meet or exceed the requirements of the vast majority of craftsmen.

Since there are still small family shops operating in Japan, it is possible to have limited numbers of special-purpose blades made from tempered-steel blanks. This can mean hand scraping, tapering and tensioning, as well as hand shaping and setting of special-tooth patterns. The hand-filed tooth of the expert will still not have the smoothness of a good-quality saw that has had its teeth cut by machines using properly maintained diamond cutting wheels.

Fig. 6. Hammer marks on a hand-straightened blade. This is an added feature found on the best-quality production saw blades.

Fig. 7. This diamond wheel is in position to cut saw teeth. Three complete passes of the wheel are required to form the crosscut tooth on the saw blade clamped to the machine table.

Saw Teeth

The teeth on Japanese blades are more specialized than on Western blades. There are different designs for softwoods and hardwoods in the crosscut patterns, as well as styles for cutting (obliquely) on a bias to the grain.

In the action of a crosscut saw, the points of the teeth act as knives and make two parallel cuts that sever the wood fibres. When hardwoods are cut, the uncut center "V" remaining easily breaks off into sawdust. With long fibre softwoods, this "V" may not break cleanly. Some Japanese crosscut saws have been developed with tooth patterns that include a raker tooth to clean out the kerf with a rip-tooth action. (Rip teeth act as chisels and literally plane off the wood in small curls.) This style of alternately set cutting teeth followed by a raker tooth can be found on some old log saw tooth patterns. It is also commonly used on "combination" carbide table-saw blades designed for both crosscutting and ripping.

Crosscut teeth modified for hardwood are shorter than those shown in Fig. 9, and have a substantial rake angle. These changes strengthen the tooth so that it can absorb the greater shock of cutting hardwood. The large gullet area of the soft-wood tooth pattern is not necessary as less waste is cut on each pass of a tooth during the cutting stroke.

Fig. 8. Hand-cut and filed saw teeth on a hand-forged blade (28 tpi). The tpi figure indicates the number of saw teeth per inch of blade. The amount of magnification in Figs. 8–14 varies, so a direct comparison of size cannot be made.

Fig. 9. Saw teeth on a standard backsaw (18 tpi).

Fig. 10. Saw teeth on a hardwood backsaw (25 tpi).

Fig. 11. Flame-hardened teeth for plywood or laminates. Note the darkened tips on the teeth (16 tpi).

Fig. 12. Ryoba *crosscut teeth (17 tpi).*

Fig. 13. Ryoba *rip teeth. Fig. 13 shows the size of the rip teeth at the toe of the blade* (7 tpi). *Fig. 14 shows the rip teeth at the heel of the blade* (11 tpi).

Fig. 14. Ryoba *rip teeth at heel of blade* (11 tpi).

Types of Saws

RYOBA

This is the most commonly used saw, and it has both a rip and a crosscut edge. Blade lengths range from 8 to 16 inches (20.3 to 40.6 cm). As size increases, the blade becomes thicker and the teeth become larger—in contrast to the Western saw, where a standard length saw is made with a number of differing teeth per inch (tpi) counts.

In common with the better-quality Western saw, the *ryoba* is taper ground back from the edge to reduce binding. However, the rip and crosscut edges of the *ryoba* will have the same set, so that the teeth on the back edge may score the surface already cut by the opposing edge if the back edge is allowed to enter the kerf. By sawing at a low angle, it is often possible to prevent this.

Though not as commonly used, there are also single-purpose saws called *kataba* which are essentially half a *ryoba*. The *kataba* in Fig. 16 actually has a combination tooth pattern consisting of sets of three teeth—a pair of crosscut teeth with alternate set and a rip tooth—and is designed for plywood.

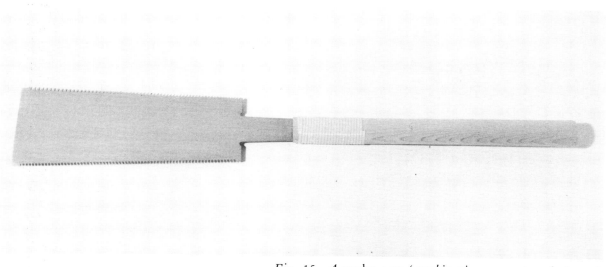

Fig. 15. A ryoba saw (combination crosscut and ripsaw).

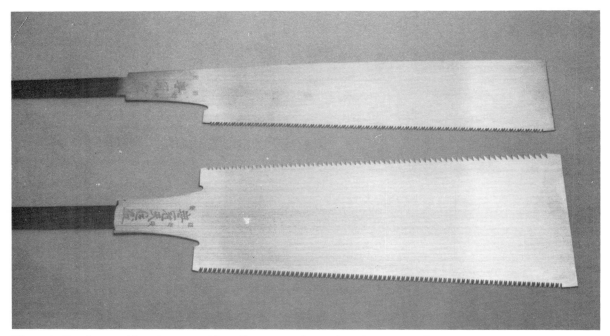

Fig. 16. Ryoba *and* kataba *saws (handles removed). A* kataba *is usually a single-purpose saw, with either a crosscut or rip tooth pattern. The* kataba *shown here has a special crosscut/rip tooth pattern.*

When starting to cut, always keep in mind the use of a low-starting angle between the blade and the work surface. This reduces the danger of overloading a single tooth by catching it on the corner of the board. To begin, guide the saw using the thumb or forefinger as a fence, and with a series of short strokes develop a definite kerf. Gradually increase the stroke length to get maximum efficiency of cut.

A close examination of the rip edge of the *ryoba* will reveal that the teeth gradually increase in size from the heel to the toe of the blade. The smaller teeth are used as starting teeth. This is similar in concept to many Western log saws which have a set of fine starting teeth at the toe of the blade.

The natural stance for the trained Japanese craftsman is to hold the workpiece with one foot and bend over while sawing. (See the wood block print on page 14.) This assures maximum control as you are pulling directly towards you.

However, for those of us not in prime physical condition, this can be an uncomfortable position. By sawing with one hand, it is possible to use a stance more natural to the Western trained sawyer. However, more control can usually be gained by using two hands spaced widely apart on the handle as shown in Fig. 19. The cutting angle should always be low enough to maintain at least three teeth in contact with the work. Figs. 20 to 28 show how to cut a tenon with a *ryoba*.

Fig. 17. The normal stance for the Japanese craftsman while crosscutting with a ryoba.

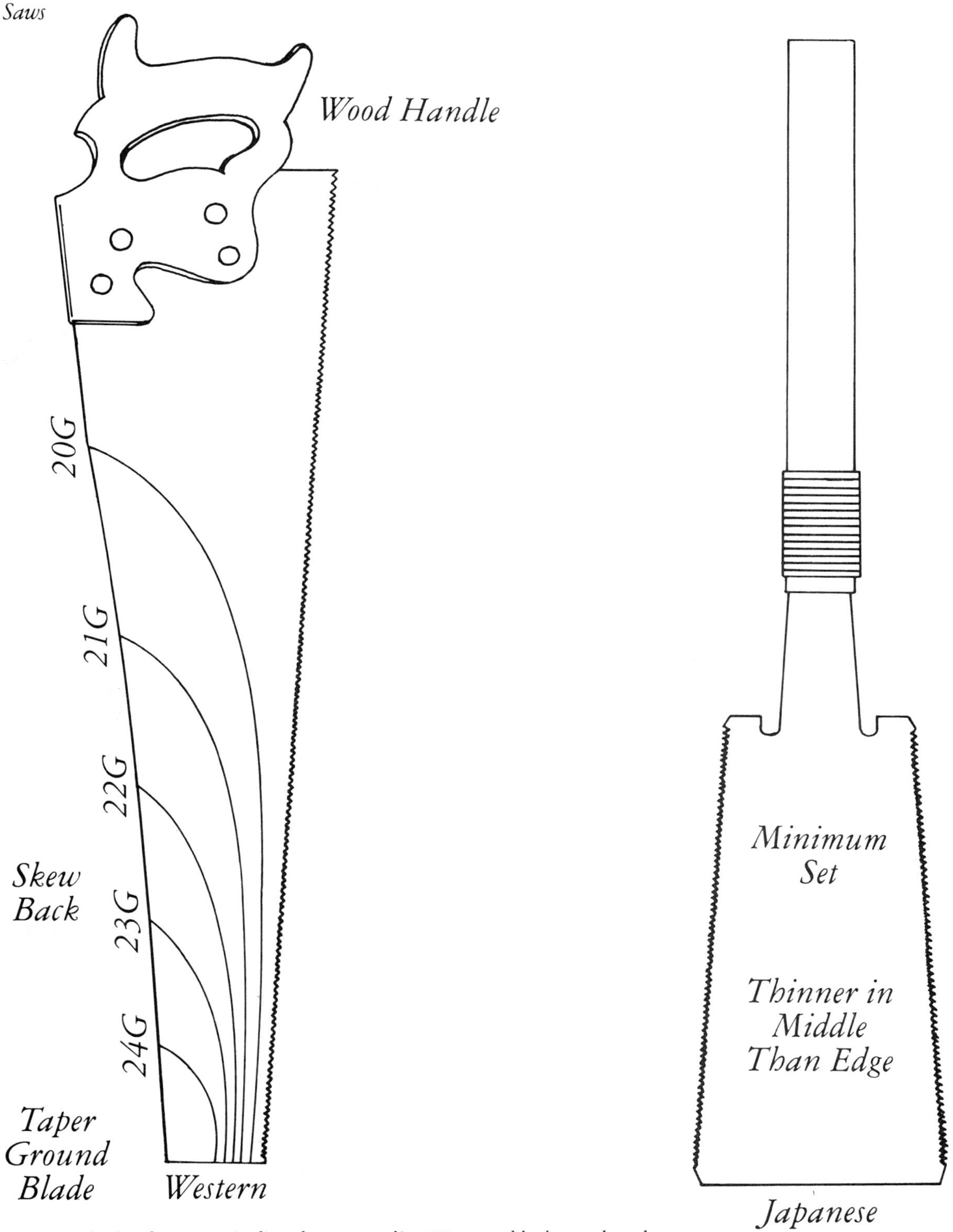

Wood Handle

20G

21G

22G

Skew
Back

23G

24G

Taper
Ground
Blade   Western

Minimum
Set

Thinner in
Middle
Than Edge

Japanese

Fig. 18. Methods of taper grinding better quality Western blades and ryoba
*blades. G is thickness of the blade expressed in metal gauge units. A higher
number is a thinner gauge. (Courtesy of Garret Wade Company.)*

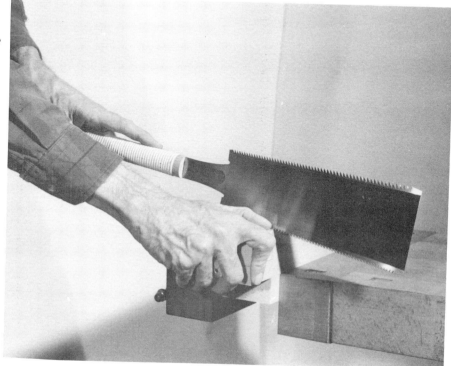

Fig. 19 (top). This ryoba is being used to crosscut with the workpiece in a bench vise. The modified two-hand grip shown allows the saw handle to be pulled past the body. The more conventional two-handed grip forces the saw handle to be pulled directly towards the user's stomach.

Fig. 20. Cutting a tenon with a ryoba: The starting cut of the shoulder is made using the crosscut side of the blade. The thumb is used as a fence to guide the blade. See Figs. 21 to 28.

Fig. 21. Cutting a tenon with a ryoba: *Cutting down the far side.*

Fig. 22. Cutting a tenon with a ryoba: *Cutting down the near side (the workpiece has been rotated 180 degrees for ease in cutting).*

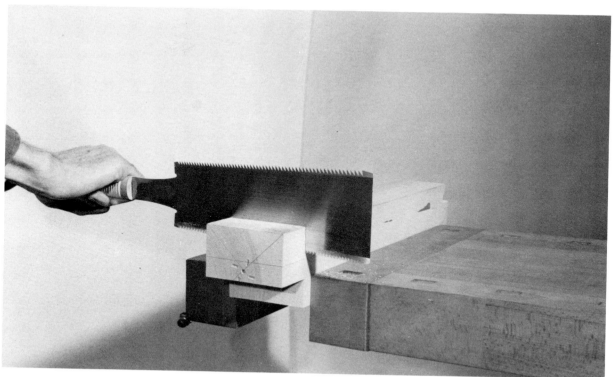

Fig. 23. Cutting a tenon with a ryoba: *Cutting down the center.*

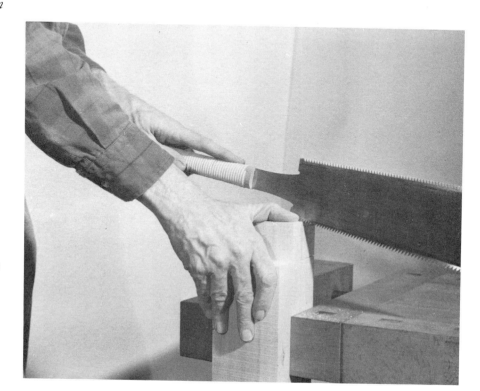

Fig. 24. Cutting a tenon with a ryoba: *Here the intersecting cut is started from the end of the tongue, using the smallest rip teeth at the heel of the blade.*

Fig. 25. *Cutting a tenon with a* ryoba: *Cutting down the far side of the tongue.*

Fig. 26. *Cutting a tenon with a* ryoba: *Cutting down the near side of the tongue.*

Fig. 27. Cutting a tenon with a ryoba: *Cutting down the center of the tongue.*

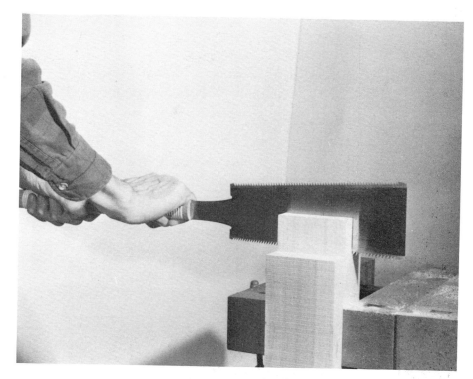

Fig. 28. Cutting a tenon with a ryoba: *The final few strokes are made with the crosscut side of the saw on the shoulder to complete the intersection of the two cuts.*

ANAHIKI

When beams or planks have to be cut, a coarser saw having a curved blade is used. It commonly ranges in size from 13 inches (33.0 cm), 8 tpi to 18 inches (45.7 cm), 5 tpi. For an equivalent length, it is thicker and coarser than a *ryoba* or *kataba.* It can be used in either ripping or crosscutting.

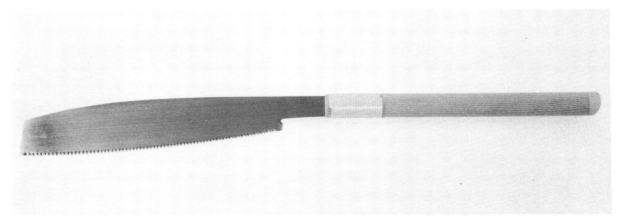

Fig. 29. Roughing saw (anahiki).

DOZUKI

The Japanese tenon or backsaw is known as a *dozuki,* and ranges in length from 8 to 11 inches (20.3 to 27.9 cm). As the teeth are very fine (18 to 28 tpi) and quite hard, most present-day production models are made with a replaceable blade. Very fine handmade versions are made with as many as 28 tpi and a blade thickness of about .014 inch. These are delicate and should only be considered for use by a craftsman with considerable experience and confidence. A saw of this quality would usually be returned to its maker for resharpening.

The standard *dozuki* blade is about 2 inches (5.1 cm) deep and comes in many tooth patterns. The traditional saw has teeth designed for fast cutting in softwoods. Smaller tooth shapes are used with hardwoods. For reinforced plastic laminates or plywoods, flame- or induction-hardened teeth can be used. These are identified by the blued tips of the teeth. The softwood pattern modified with various raker patterns is a recent introduction. By removing the waste remaining, the raker teeth action allows the regular teeth to cut more rapidly by cutting more deeply on each stroke of the saw.

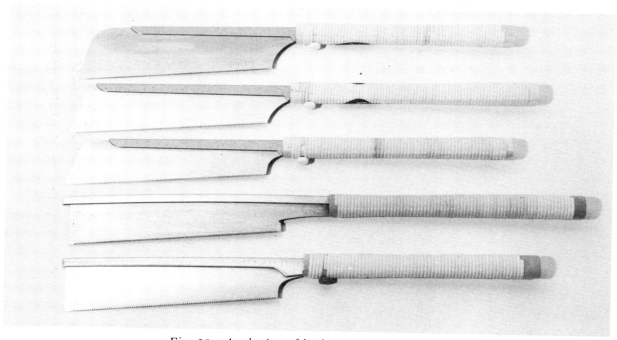

Fig. 30. A selection of backsaws (dozuki). *From top to bottom: standard, hardwood, plywood, hand-forged hardwood, and hardwood with raker pattern teeth. (Note: All saws shown, with the exception of the hand-forged blade, have quick-change replaceable blades secured by the locking knob on the lower side of the handle.)*

Fig. 31. Folding blade dozuki. The cutting edge of the blade folds into a groove in the handle to protect the saw teeth when the saw is carried in a tool box.

The *dozuki* is usually held in one hand. The beginner will obtain the most control by gripping the middle of the handle and extending the first finger along the top pointing towards the spine of the blade. See Fig. 32. Start the cut using only the front one-third of the blade and with a series of short strokes develop a definite kerf. Gradually lengthen the stroke, taking care to pull straight to reduce the possibility of the saw catching on the return stroke and kinking or even shattering the blade.

As an aid in beginning a cut, many Japanese will use gauge blocks of wood as a fence for the blade to ride against. Since they are of wood, they do not harm the saw teeth. These blocks can be purchased precut, but the craftsman can easily make his own.

When cutting joints or tenons, it will be easier to mark all three sides of the cut and make a series of cuts in three steps for the greatest accuracy. If it is a shallow cut, first cut down to the desired depth on the far side, then the near side. Finally, the triangle left over in the middle is cut down to match the sides. For deeper cuts, make a series of such cuts. See Fig. 34.

If a replaceable blade has a tendency to slip from the back spine, remove the blade from the bar and carefully narrow the opening of the slot in a machinist's vise that has smooth steel or fibre-faced jaws. To reseat the blade, simply rap the back of the bar on a block of wood.

Fig. 32. Starting a cut with a dozuki *using thumb as a fence.*

Fig. 33. Starting a cut with a dozuki *using a wooden mitre fence.*

Fig. 34. Sequence of 3 different blade angles for greatest accuracy when sawing tenon. Figs. 25–27 illustrate this sequence.

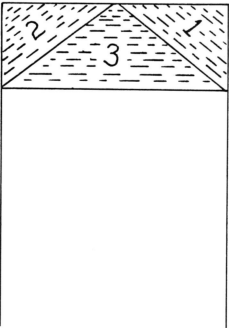

DOVETAIL SAW

For the cabinetmaker cutting a dovetail, a saw with a shorter and deeper blade than the standard *dozuki* will offer more control. This saw is a recent development for the Western market, as the small dovetail is not a normal Japanese construction joint in cabinetry. This saw has a blade 7¼ x 2 inches (18.4 cm x 5.1 cm) with a modified rip-tooth pattern so that it will cut efficiently in either hardwood or softwood on a bias to the wood grain. The traditional Japanese saw most comparable to this design is the *hosobiki*.

There is another still shorter steel-backed blade called a *shitaji* which is used for slotting. The blade is about 6 inches long x 1 inch deep (15.2 cm x 2.5 cm) and can be very useful in the cutting of small mitres.

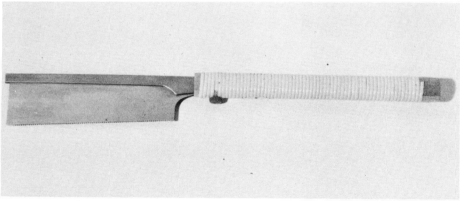

Fig. 35. Backsaw designed for dovetails.

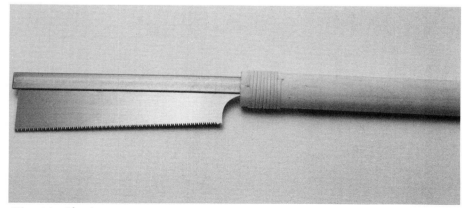

Fig. 36. Slotting saw .

SPECIALTY SAWS

Another traditional Japanese blade that has been reintroduced is the *kugihiki* or flush-cutting saw. It has a blade which tapers from heel to toe and is designed to cut off a plug or dowel flush with the work surface. As it has no set to the teeth, it will not mar the surface of the surrounding wood. The flexibility of the thin tapered blade allows the handle to be bent away from the work surface while the blade is forced into a flush contact to ensure a level cut.

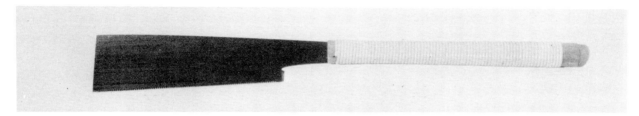

Fig. 37. Flush-cutting saw with a tapered blade.

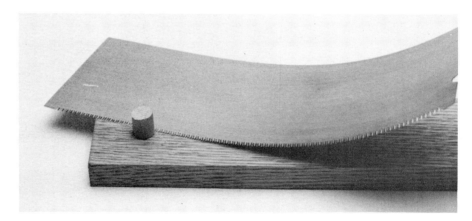

Fig. 38. Flush-cutting saw in use trimming a dowel.

The *azebiki* is a small *ryoba*-type saw which has a short blade with curved edges that allow the user to begin a cut in the center of a panel. This blade is slightly larger than a Western veneer saw and it has a much longer neck between blade and handle. This is necessary in order to provide hand clearance when making a deep cut, which is not a problem when cutting veneers. See Fig. 39.

Fine compass and keyhole saws are also available. Since they cut on the pull stroke, they are not as susceptible to the bending and kinking so common to their Western equivalents.

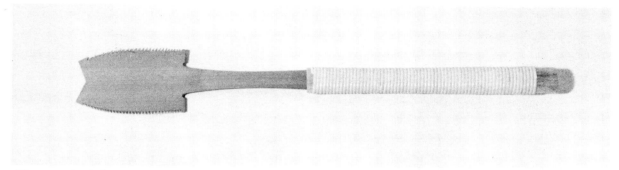

Fig. 39. Azebiki.

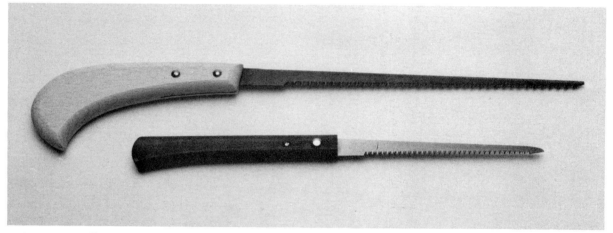

Fig. 40. Small trim saw (top) and compass saw (bottom).

How to Sharpen Saws

Because Japanese saws have such a fine pitch, it is usually more economical to replace a blade than to have it sharpened and reset. Resharpening can be done by using extremely fine diamond-shaped files, which range in length from 2 to 7 inches (5.1 to 14.8 cm) and in cross sections from 1/16 inch x 3/8 inch (1 mm x 9.5 mm) and up. Expensive saws are commonly returned to the maker for resharpening. In Japan, I have seen saws that had been resharpened so many times that they were half their original width.

The position of the saw filer can be seen in the carving shown in Fig. 2. The saw depicted is an old logging saw. For smaller hand saws, a wooden vise is used to clamp the blade. This fixture would then traditionally be held firmly against a wooden block by the feet, leaving both hands free for filing.

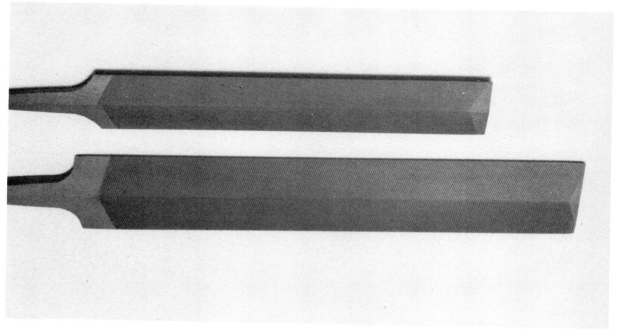

Fig. 41. Thin, diamond-shaped files are used for sharpening dozuki *and* ryoba *saws. The lengths for the files shown are 3″ and 4″ (7.6 cm and 10.2 cm).*

II · SHARPENING STONES

Over the years, many sources of natural stone have been used for sharpening. Some of the more common types include sandstone, Welsh slate, Belgian block, Arkansas novaculites, garnet, diamond particles and, of more interest here, Japanese waterstones.

Like sandstone, the best Japanese stones are sedimentary rock. Unlike sandstone, they are not readily cut from open quarries but must be mined from shafts deep in the ground. While certain stones such as the Arkansas cut best in conjunction with a light oil, sandstone and the soft stones from Belgium and Japan cut best when used with water. The dense,

Fig. 42. This natural stone is a medium-quality sharpening stone. (Note the different sediment layers in the formation of the stone.)

more crystalline structure of the quartzite Arkansas stone is a granular form of pure silica rock formed by the metamorphism of sandstone under heat and pressure. Thus, some form of sandstone appears in most commonly used natural sharpening stones.

Japanese sharpening stones range from clay-like compounds similar to tripoli that come from open pit mines to the chalk-like dressing stones to the fine Awase finishing stones found only by mining narrow veins in mines.

In the course of trying to separate myth from reality concerning Japanese stones, I visited a mine located a short distance from Kyoto, the old capital of Japan. This mine had been worked for more than 1,200 years, and its entrance was located far up the side of a steep wooded hillside. Entering the main shaft of the mine with only my hand-held carbide lamp as a guide, I had to walk with bent knees and bowed head to keep from hitting the roof as my shoulders rubbed the sides of the walls. After walking in this fashion for about 10 minutes, I reached an enlarged gallery from which shafts branched off in various directions and followed different veins of usable rock. These veins are usually not more than a few inches wide. Different areas of the mine will produce different qualities of stone.

From the mine, the usable stone is transported to a cutting shop where it is graded for fineness, purity and size. Grading is subjective. Experts have different reasons for buying a particular type of stone. Among the factors considered important are: whether the tool to be sharpened is being used by a carpenter, cabinetmaker or temple builder; whether a cabinetmaker working with hardwoods prefers a harder stone; or whether an extremely hard blade would need a softer stone.

The blue "Ao" stone is a general-purpose cutting stone used for general sharpening. The finer Awase finishing stone can range in price from $20 to $2,000 for stones of equal size. Even price is no certainty of quality, as the best stone may contain a defect in its interior. Most are not perfect rectangles, but will have broken corners. Ultimate selection is largely based on the buyer following the advice and biases of mentors

and blade makers, plus his own experiences. To the unini-
tiated, there may be little perceptible difference in the cutting
action between a $75 and a $1,500 stone. The top prices are
for light cream-color stones which are constant in their cutting action. These characteristics are the result of the purity
and fineness of the active cutting particles.

Man-Made Stones

Artificial waterstones of aluminum oxide were developed
about 50 years ago but, in Japan, it was only after World War
II that usage became widespread. Artificial abrasives have now
developed to the state that low-priced, uniform particle-size
cutting stones are readily available in a wide range of grits.
Grit sizes were once determined by sifting particles through a
mesh screen. Size would be the number of screen openings per
linear inch of screen. See Fig. 44.

*Fig. 43. Man-made stones. From left to right: 250/1000 grit combination,
1000 grit, 6000 grit, and 8000 grit.*

Comparison of Sharpening Stones Grit Size in Microns

Oilstone (approx.)	Grit	Micron Range
Medium India	240	87.5–73.5
Fine Crystolon	280	73.5–62
	320	62.0–52.5
	360	52.5–44
	400	44.0–37
	500	37.0–31
	600	31.0–26
Fine India	700	26.0–22
	800	22.0–18
	1000	18.0–14.5
Soft Arkansas	1200	14.5–11.5
Hard Arkansas	1500	11.5–8.9
	2000	8.9–7.1
	2500	7.1–5.9
Black Hard Arkansas	3000	5.9–4.7
	4000	3.5–2.5
	6000	2.5–1.5
Lapping Compound	8000	1.5–0.5

One Micron = 1/1000 millimetre

50 microns= .05mm= .002″=dia. of human hair

Fig. 44. Grit sizes for sharpening stones.

The coarsest stones ranging from 50 to 120 grit are of grey silicon carbide made from fused silica sand and coke. The finer stones of silicon carbide to about 220 grit are green in color. Stones from 700 to 1200 grit are of aluminum oxide with a porous ceramic binder formed by baking a mixture of clays under high heat and pressure. Finishing stones, also usually of aluminum oxide and with grits from 4000 to 8000, have a porous synorogenic resin binder and are formed under much lower temperatures.

Other man-made abrasives for use with both water and oil have been made by grinding natural stone and reconstituting it with a binder. Examples can be found of Arkansas, Belgium and Japanese stones being made by this process. As with natural stones, any synthetic stone made by this procedure can exhibit a nonuniform cutting action if the abrasive particles are not of equal fineness and purity.

In buying any stone, the only true indicator of its quality is the reputation of the manufacturer.

Stone Selection

In Japan, most finishing operations by chisel makers are done on large horizontal, powered wheels using man-made stones. For the final polishing, they may use such varied methods as natural stones, man-made stones or lapping on a steel plate or on a revolving wooden wheel.

Traditionalists who have been indoctrinated through long training and use say that only a natural stone can produce a superior edge. A more current opinion is that the best polish can come from a final pass on a natural stone, but experts question whether this produces a keener or longer-lasting cutting edge.

Sharpening is an art that's learned through practice and patience. For those of us who have not developed these skills, lapping compounds, strops, 8000 grit stones or a $2,000 natural stone are not going to produce a superior edge. In Japan, they recommend a 1000 grit stone for use on the average carpenter's tools. For a better quality edge, the 4000 grit stone is usually sufficient.

One method used to test the sharpness of a cutting edge is to run the edge lightly over the hair on your forearm. If the hair is cut, the edge is sharp enough. In instances when you are looking for an edge this sharp, the 8000 grit stone or a lapping system will probably have to be used.

In recent years, Japanese manufacturers have introduced motorized versions of their synthetic waterstones. Unlike the traditional Western-mechanized sandstone wheel, which is mounted vertically while cutting on its circumference, the Japanese units are spun on a vertical axis, and the side of the wheel is used in cutting. This produces a flat or even slightly convex bevel that is much stronger than the "hollow grind" produced by small diameter vertical wheels. Available stones for these systems range from 100 to 8000 grit and can be augmented by steel-lapping plates and hard felt discs. While the units seen in the United States and Europe commonly have an 8-inch (20.3-cm) diameter wheel, those used in production flattening and grinding in Japan are as wide as 36 inches (91.4 cm).

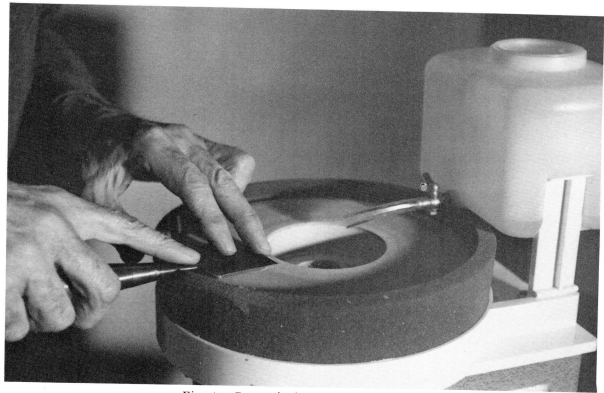

Fig. 45. Powered whetstone grinder being used to flatten back of a chisel.

The Use of Japanese Waterstones

These stones are very porous and are designed to be used with water as a lubricant and cleansing agent. In general, synthetic cutting stones should be saturated with water before use and then stored in a container of water or a closed form-fitting plastic box so that they can easily be made ready for use. Starting with a dry stone, it takes about 15 minutes of immer-

sion to properly soak a stone. Continuous immersion is not required for the finer 4000-to-8000 grit finishing stones, as they
absorb water rapidly. Under no circumstance should a natural
Japanese waterstone be continuously stored in water or, like
sandstone, it will disintegrate.

As you begin to work a tool over the well-wetted surface of
the stone, the water and loosened stone fragments will produce a slurry (a water mixture of insoluble matter). The water
flushes away the swarf (debris) and keeps new sharp particles
exposed for a fast-cutting action. In the sharpening process,
the abrasive particles are crushed and produce an even finer
grit.

When you are ready to change to a finer grit stone, let the
slurry build up; add just enough water to maintain fluidity,
and keep the stone surface moist while reducing working
pressure on the tool being sharpened. This slows the sharpening action and reduces the depth of the abrasion marks on
the tool surface, which allows you to achieve a finer finish
faster during the succeeding stage. If the stone surface is allowed to become too dry, iron particles will become imbedded
in the stone surface.

Before moving on to a finer stone, wipe clean the tool
being sharpened so that particles from the coarser stone will
not be transferred to the finer stone.

On finishing stones, initially rubbing with a dressing stone
on the surface will build up a slurry quicker than the action of
passing the tool to be sharpened over the stone. This step will
also produce a faster cutting action. The dressing stone can
also be used to renew the surface of a stone that has become
glazed over.

In the United States, these chalk-like dressing stones are
commonly known as Nagura stones, a name that stems from
their Kyoto origins. In Japan, they have many other names
which are used to identify the region in which they are found
or are used. Names include *Numata* (Toyko), *Amakusa* (Na-
gasaki) and *Io* (Shikoko). Artificial dressing stones are now
produced and are often included with 8000 grit stones.

Fig. 46. Synthetic stone (left) and natural stone.

During the sharpening process, use the full surface of the stone and occasionally change the stone from end to end to promote even wear. Japanese waterstones wear faster than oilstones—in fact, this is the reason for their faster cutting action. New abrasive cutting particles are continuously being exposed.

From time to time it will be necessary to reflatten the stone. A traditional Japanese method is simply to wet the stone thoroughly and rub it over another flat stone or even a concrete surface. Ideally, a stone should be flattened by rubbing it together with a similar stone so that no contamination is possible. A good method for truing is to place a sheet of 220-grit wet/dry silicon-carbide paper on a true, flat surface such as a piece of plate glass or machined steel, flood it with water, and work the stone across the abrasive sheet. When a dissimilar material is used to true a stone, it is important to clean the surface before using.

The coarser waterstones usually do not come mounted on a wooden base. To prevent slippage during use, they can be placed on a sheet of soft rubber or a wet towel. Alternatively, a simple wooden jig can be made which will allow you to clamp the stone in a vise or bridge it across a sink. If you decide to do your sharpening over a sink, keep in mind that the swarf can easily clog the drain trap and, being composed of sand and metal particles, will not easily dissolve.

An additional word of caution: If you allow a wet waterstone to freeze, it may very well spall or fracture.

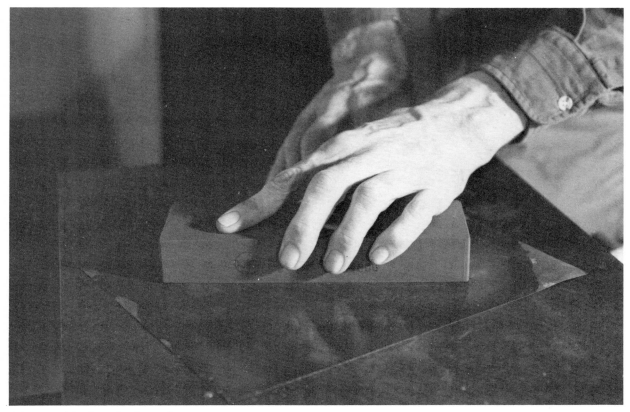

Fig. 47. Truing the face of a 1000 grit stone using silicon-carbide paper and water on a ground cast-iron table.

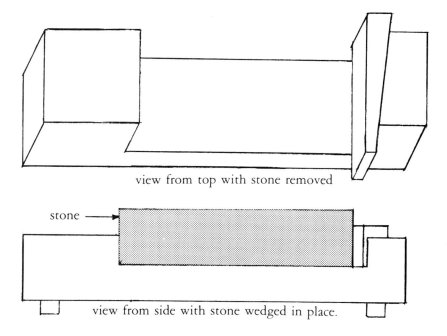

view from top with stone removed

stone →

view from side with stone wedged in place.

Fig. 48. This simple wooden base can be constructed for a waterstone. The tapered wedge locks the stone to the base. The runners on the bottom of the base can be used as inside or outside stops when the base is used over a pan of water. If the block is to be clamped in a vise, the base should be constructed in a "T" shape; the vertical member of the "T" will provide a clamping surface.

III · PLANES

The most difficult of the commonly used Japanese wood-working tools for the Western craftsman to adapt to is the plane. A photograph of a smoothing plane at the finish of a long pass with a continuous length of tissue-thin shaving curling behind it serves as an introduction to many articles on Japanese planes. However, the work to condition the plane to perform this cut and the continual hand tuning necessary to do this can be extremely time-consuming. For a person not committed to using Japanese tools exclusively or who will only be using a plane at odd intervals, a Japanese plane is probably not a good choice.

A closer look at that piece of wood from which a tissue-thin shaving was cut will probably reveal a clear, straight-grained softwood such as Japanese cedar or cypress. An examination of the plane body shows it to be made from a single block of red or white oak that has been extensively cut away at the blade seat and throat, which makes this section very prone to twist. As with any unlaminated piece of wood, it will have a tendency to move with changes in climatic conditions. To overcome this, the best wooden planes from Europe have a lignum vitae sole laminated to a beech-wood body by use of a keyed joint cut on a bias to the grain. While this stabilizes the shorter planes, a long jointer plane can bow noticeably under wide variations in humidity.

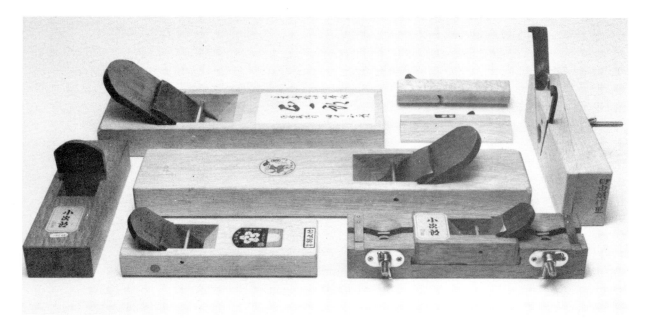

Fig. 49. A selection of general-purpose Japanese planes.

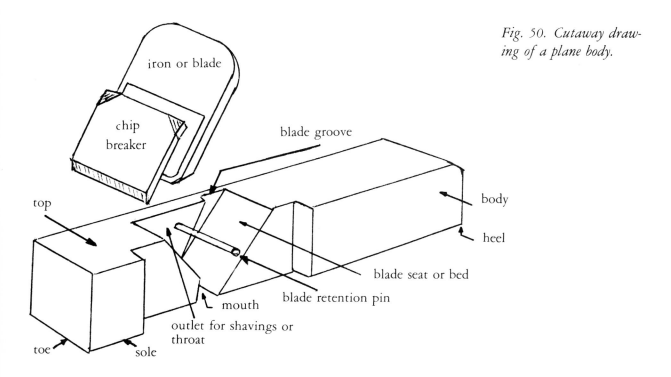

Fig. 50. Cutaway drawing of a plane body.

It is possible that in Japan their particular plane design evolved into the precise instrument it is because it is often the last tool used in finishing the surface of the workpiece. In contrast to Western craftsmanship, no scraping, sanding or protective finishing is likely to be done. There is no doubt that a properly performing Japanese plane is a fast, smooth-cutting tool that can be a pleasure to use. However, to arrive at that state of perfection can require many hours of preliminary work.

Preparing the Plane for Use

SEATING THE BLADE

While it is possible to purchase the plane block and blade separately or to even make the block, most people will begin by purchasing a plane which is complete except for the final seating of the blade and conditioning of the sole. Without doing this, any attempt to seat the blade in a cutting position on a new plane can cause the body to split or make blade removal extremely difficult. In many instances, this condition is aggravated by the climatic changes between the dampness of Japan and the often hot, dry air to be found in many American storerooms and shops. This difference may already have caused the plane block to shrink around the blade and freeze it in place. If this has occurred, the safest way to remove the blade is to set the plane aside for several weeks in a cool, relatively humid location to allow the wood to swell and relieve the pressure that is holding the blade.

The blade is removed by striking the top edge of the block behind the blade. Before starting, make sure that this edge is well-rounded or even has a slight chamfer. Hold the plane in one hand with your index finger pushing up on the blade, while alternately striking on either side of the centerline of the back edge to loosen the blade. With the index finger it is possible to feel the blade loosening, as well as prevent the blade from popping out unexpectedly.

To be most effective, the force of the hammer blow must be applied in a line which is parallel to the plane of the blade. See Fig. 51. Don't strike the corners or the back face of the block. Not striking the edge squarely or striking the corner can cause the block to split. Striking the back face wastes most of the effective force of the blow.

The procedure will have to be followed each time the blade is to be removed. In replacing the blade, note that the hollow-ground side of the blade faces upwards.

For the blade to be seated properly, it must be fitted to the groove in the throat of the block. All fitting must be done on the plane seat and the sides of the groove, as the upper surface determines the cutting angle of the blade.

Remove the chip breaker. With the chip breaker removed, find the location of the high spots that prevent the blade from being pushed down into the mouth. To do this, cover the edges and back of the blade with soft graphite pencil or slow-drying ink from a felt-tipped pen. While the ink is still wet, seat the blade firmly in its groove by tapping lightly with a hammer. Immediately remove the blade as described previously.

Fig. 51. Remove the blade by striking the back edge with a hammer.

On those areas where the blade has made contact with the block, the ink will have been transferred to the wood. See Fig. 52. Pare or scrape the ink from these areas. It may be easier to do this if the chip-breaker retaining pin has been removed. Repeat this process until the blade can be positioned with its cutting edge just emerging from the mouth of the plane. In this position the blade should not be bound tightly by the sides of the groove but should have about 1/32-inch (1-mm) clearance on each side to allow for lateral blade adjustment. If necessary, the sides of the groove can be opened by using a small saw and a narrow chisel.

In the initial seating of the blade, if too much of the wood has been pared away or the blade has been used a great deal, the blade protrudes too far through the mouth. The damage can be repaired by gluing a thin piece of paper onto the blade seat.

With the blade seated and the chip breaker in place about 1/64 inch behind the cutting edge, check the opening of the mouth. Ideally, it should be slightly wider than the shaving to be cut and even from side to side. The mouth should open

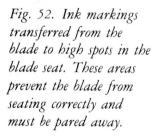

Fig. 52. Ink markings transferred from the blade to high spots in the blade seat. These areas prevent the blade from seating correctly and must be pared away.

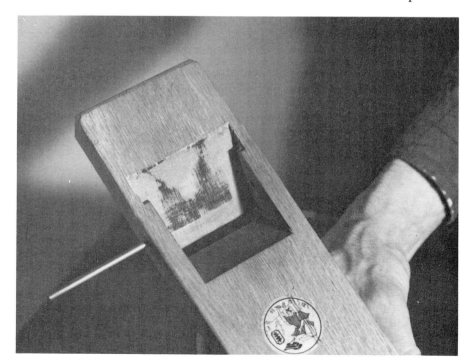

Fig. 53. Scrape away the high spots with a chisel. Note that the retaining pin has been pulled out of the way.

Fig. 54. Sight along the plane bottom when adjusting the blade-cutting position with a hammer.

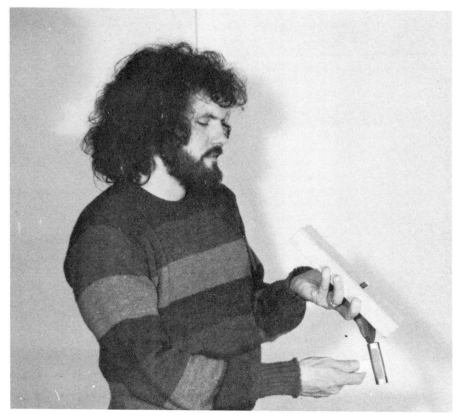

Fig. 55. Pare the side of the blade groove with a chisel to provide necessary side clearance for the blade.

gradually as it enters the throat of the plane body. See Fig. 63.

Note that only the blade and not the chip breaker protrudes from the mouth. Also note the slight chamfer on the sole behind the blade cutting edge. These details will be explained on page 60.

CONDITIONING THE SOLE

Since the stability of the plane block is affected by changes in climatic conditions, the sole must be checked for flatness and twist before use. To do this, use a straightedge and check lengthwise on the diagonals and crosswise while marking the high spots.

Fig. 56. Use the straightedge to check the plane bottom for flatness.

Fig. 57. Use the straightedge to check the plane bottom for twist.

Another way to find the high spots is to use a true, flat reference such as a ground plate glass. Coat it with a thin film of a carbon black solution. Then while holding the plane firmly, run it over the surface of the plate so that the high spots will pick up the blacking. The same procedure can be followed using a piece of pencil carbon paper on the reference flat, but it is hard to keep the paper from tearing or wrinkling.

The marked high spots are then removed by scraping across the grain with a scraping plane or a wide chisel held vertically. See Figs. 60 and 61. When doing this, have the blade in place but just slightly withdrawn into the mouth. If the sole is trued with the blade removed, reseating the blade will cause the area immediately under the blade to bulge out slightly from the pressure exerted by tapping the blade into place.

Fig. 58. Check for twist and flatness with a piece of carbon paper on plate glass. Make sure the plate glass is supported on a flat surface.

Fig. 59. *The carbon from the paper has been transferred to the high points on the plane bottom.*

Fig. 60. *Scraping the plane bottom with a chisel. Scraping techniques with both the chisel and the scraping plane (see Fig. 61) are used for flattening and adding "wave" pattern.*

Fig. 61. Scraping the plane bottom with a scraping plane.

The traditional Japanese craftsman will now further modify the sole by creating a wave pattern so that there are only a few contact lines about 1/16 inch wide between the plane bottom and the workpiece. The most common pattern has the plane sole making contact only at the front edge and just in front of the mouth with a 1/64-inch to 1/32-inch-high arched relief or wave in between. The remainder of the sole behind the blade starts with a slight relief of .004 inch to .008 inch, expanding to about 1/64 inch at the back edge, which in effect creates a half wave as illustrated in Fig. 62.

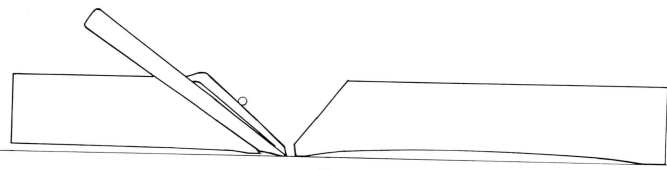

Fig. 62. Note the "wave" pattern on a smoothing plane.

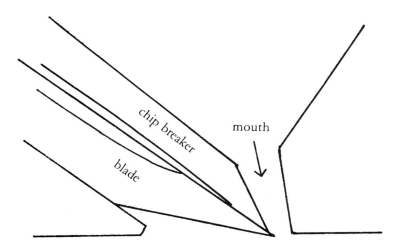

Fig. 63. A look at the relative positions of the blade and chip breaker. Note the blunted edge of the mouth behind the blade.

These dimensions will vary depending upon whether the plane is used for roughing or smoothing. For added control, some planes will also have a line of contact at the back edge, or—especially on the longer jointer plane—2 separate waves broken by a line of contact in front of the blade.

By tradition, the amount of relief is designated as one paper thick just behind the cutting edge and two papers thick at the center of the wave and at the trailing edge.

Finishing touches include chamfering the sides of the sole to the blade groove width so that the length of the line of contact is only slightly more than the width of the blade itself. The sharp leading edge of the mouth under the blade should be given a ½₂-inch chamfer. This eliminates a sharp edge that could either splinter in use or pick up a wood splinter springing up after being compressed by the cutting action of the iron. The final touch is a small triangular cut from the outside corner of the front of the blade groove at the mouth, angling down across the width to about ½₂ inch at the back edge of the groove.

As the sole wears from use or twists due to aging or warping, it must be reconditioned as required if the plane is to perform to its optimum capabilities.

Fig. 64. The transition cut is made at the corners of the blade mouth.

Fig. 65. This well-tuned plane is being used on a clear, straight-grained soft-wood board. The board surface has been slightly moistened to assist in the formation of continuous shaving.

SHARPENING THE PLANE BLADE

The heart of the Japanese plane is the massive tapered blade, which is about ⅜ inch (9.5 mm) thick at its upper end. Although there are still blade makers in Japan who can hand forge blades, most of the better quality blades are hammer-forged and machine-ground. As a result, they are relatively flat. However, a new blade should be checked for flatness on the hollow ground face. If it is not true, it must be lapped on a soft steel plate with silicon-carbon powder and water. Grits are readily available in a range from 50 to 600 mesh size. Starting particle size will depend upon the amount of material to be removed.

Begin lapping by placing about half a teaspoon of grit on the plate with enough water to obtain a good grit distribution as you lap. Using even pressure, rub the blade back and forth over the plate while holding the blade perpendicular to the plate. When heavy lapping is required, better control and higher pressure can be maintained by laying a length of wood across the top of the blade and grasping the ends as handles using the thumb and forefinger to stabilize the blade. See Fig. 70.

As lapping proceeds, occasionally wipe off the blade to see if a uniform pattern has been established. The quickest way to obtain a fine finish is, at this point, to wash the lapping plate and blade free of the grit being used and move on to a finer grade. A final lap with 600-grit powder will give a mirror-like finish. A grey or matte surface can be as smooth as a mirror surface. A mirror surface is more difficult to achieve and will more readily show scratches.

The sharpening process can now be continued on a stone. The selection of a starting stone will depend upon the condition of the cutting edge. If the blade is badly nicked, it will be easier if you first obtain a true edge by flattening the end of the blade to the depth of the flaw. Be sure to hold the blade in a vertical position while doing this. See Fig. 71.

For extensive regrinding, start with a 100- or 220-grit sliconcarbide stone. For normal resharpening, an 800- or 1000-grit stone can be used initially.

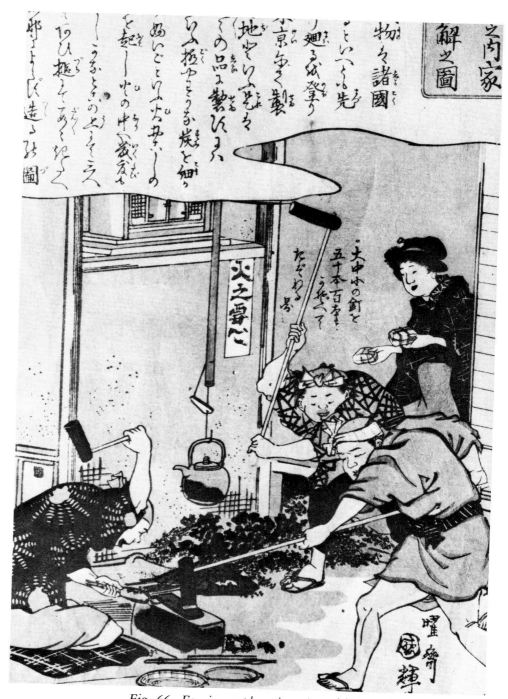

Fig. 66. Forging a plane iron (wood block print, circa 1870).

Fig. 67. This master smith is sizing a hand-forged blade. (Courtesy of Uozumi, from Miki City.)

Fig. 68. The stages in a blade-forging process. From top left: plane blade blank of wrought-iron body and hard steel insert before lamination, through the forging, heat treatment, and grinding processes to the finished blade.

Fig. 69. Add silicon-car-
bide powder to the sur-
face of the soft-steel
lapping plate before flattening the back of the
blade.

Fig. 70. Lapping blade
with a wooden pressure
bar.

Fig. 71. Lap the back of a blade with a revolving flat steel plate on a whetstone grinder.

In sharpening, the most important factor is to maintain a constant bevel angle and uniform pressure while traversing the stone surface. If you do not feel confident in doing this, there is a honing guide designed for Japanese blades that will make it easier. See Figs. 72 and 73. Otherwise, find a grip that is comfortable and positive and proceed to sharpen in the same manner as with a Western blade. A suggested method is to establish the bevel angle by holding the cutting edge firmly against the stone using the middle fingers of the left hand. Then grasp the blade with the right hand placing the thumb on the edge under the left hand, and the index finger on the right-hand corner of the blade cutting edge. With cutting stones (as opposed to finishing stones), it is easier to apply more pressure correctly if the blade is held at an angle to the stone.

As you sharpen the blade, the line of light at the dull edge will gradually disappear and a slight wire edge will form on the back of the blade. This can be felt by rubbing the thumb or finger up the back across the end of the blade. At this point, move to a finishing stone and continue working on the bevel-cutting edge until it has a uniform smoothness. Then turn the blade over, and with the blade flat on the stone and perpendicular to its length, rub the blade back and forth until the wire edge disappears.

As with Western planes, ideally a finishing blade should have its cutting edge slightly rounded (and a roughing plane even more so) to keep the corners of the blade from digging into the work surface. This is done by alternately varying pressure at the opposite corners of the cutting bevel during the sharpening process. On a finishing plane, it is also possible to leave the edge straight but radius the corners.

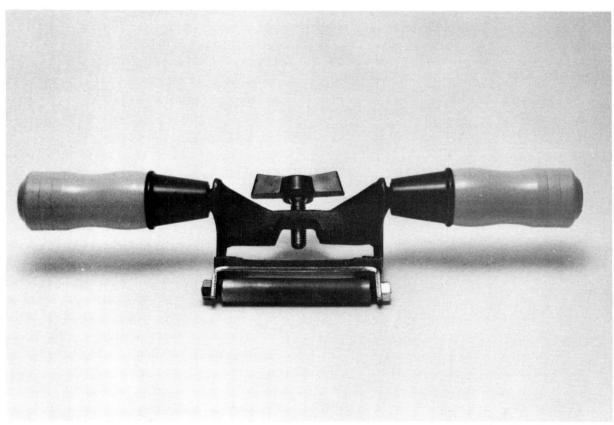

Fig. 72. Honing guide.

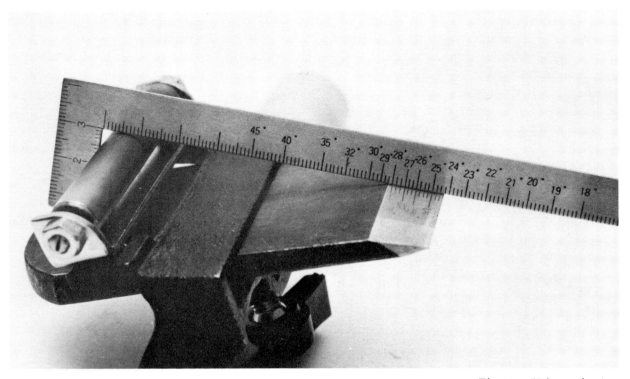

Fig. 73. Using a honing guide rule to measure the cutting bevel angle.

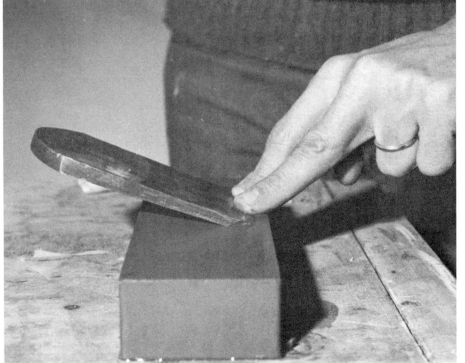

Fig. 74. Establishing the cutting bevel angle on the sharpening stone.

Fig. 75. Holding the blade for maximum control during sharpening.

Fig. 76. Stoning the back of the blade.

Fig. 77. Final passes over a finishing stone are made so that any abrasive score marks are parallel to the cutting action of the blade.

FITTING THE CHIP BREAKER

The purpose of the chip breaker is to reduce the bending stress in the wood fibres being cut, and therefore eliminate wood tear-out as these fibres approach the cutting edge. This is done by breaking the wood fibres immediately after they have been cut or raised by the cutting bevel. By positioning the bevel edge of the chip breaker just behind the cutting edge of the blade, this secondary bevel forces the cut fibres to be bent almost vertical as they pass through the plane mouth and into the throat.

To work effectively, the chip breaker must have a sharp edge and it must sit flat on the blade. Any gap would allow fine shavings to jam between the chip breaker and the blade. Fig. 78 shows the action of a cutting edge with and without the chip breaker.

The chip breaker is sharpened in the same manner as the main blade. When positioned in the plane body, the chip

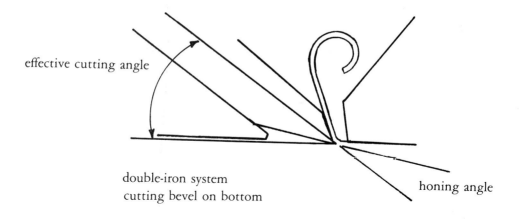

effective cutting angle

honing angle

double-iron system
cutting bevel on bottom

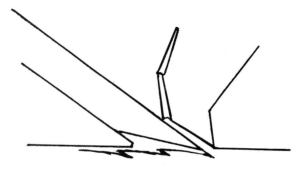

cutting bevel on bottom—(no chip breaker)

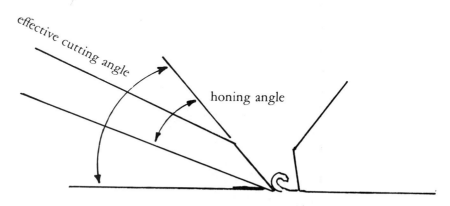

effective cutting angle

honing angle

single-iron system
cutting bevel on top (no chip breaker)

Fig. 78. Cutting edge with or without the chip breaker.

Fig. 79. Fitting the chip breaker to the plane iron.

breaker is held against the blade by a retaining pin which spans the width of the plane throat. If the chip breaker doesn't seat against the blade properly, it can be raised or lowered on either side by adjusting one of its top bent corners with a hammer on an anvil. If the chip breaker is too wide to reach to the mouth, the sides of the plane throat should be pared with a chisel to provide enough space so that some lateral adjustment is available to align the chip-breaker bevel edge to the main blade cutting edge.

The closer the chip breaker edge to the cutting edge, the cleaner the cut. That obviously also limits the depth of cut, and for normal operations it should be positioned about 1/64 inch behind the cutting edge. On a plane used for fine finishing, this can be reduced further. To be completely effective, the chip breaker must be slightly wider than the cutting edge.

Using the Plane

With the plane components ready for use, replace the main blade, the hollow-ground side up, into its groove and set it to the desired cutting depth by tapping the top of the blade with a hammer. The best way to determine the cutting depth of the blade is to hold the plane upside down with one hand while sighting down the sole against a light-colored background. With a hammer in the other hand, it is possible to extend the blade or adjust for parallelism by tapping the top of the blade from the underside. See Fig. 54. Next, insert the chip breaker, the hollow-ground side and bent corners down, and position it by tapping the top edge until it is set properly. See Fig. 80. Remember that if the main blade must be backed out the procedures detailed on page 51 should be followed.

There are circumstances in which a single-iron plane without a chip breaker can be effective. Sometimes it is necessary

Fig. 80. Positioning the chip breaker in the plane body, using a hammer for adjustment.

to plane against the grain because it reverses along the length of the workpiece or it is a "wild" grain with no regular pattern. In such cases, a high-pitch angle on the plane iron which actually removes wood more by a scraping action than a cutting action will produce the smoothest surface. In such a plane design, the single iron would be installed with the bevel angle on the top side; only a small amount of wood can be removed during a pass.

As the plane is used with a pulling stroke, the manner in which it is held must differ from the hand positions used with a traditional Western plane. For the beginner, it is easier to cup the pulling hand behind the blade while using the other hand to hold the plane against the workpiece and to guide its direction. For a person with large hands, this may cause the

Fig. 81. Holding a smoothing plane while finishing the edge of a board.

pulling hand to be pinched between the underside of the blade and the plane body. An alternative method with smoothing planes is to position the pulling hand with the first finger—and possibly the middle finger—behind the blade and the other fingers bearing against the end of the plane block.

A method for planing long boards in one continuous motion is shown in Figs. 82 to 85. For workpieces too long to be finished by this method, it is necessary to walk alongside the piece as it is being surfaced. When either of these methods is used, it is possible to eliminate any blade marks that would occur when a plane starts or stops on the board surface.

Figs. 86 to 88 show the foot position of the woodworker during planing. Figs. 89 to 91 show the hand positions during the planing of a wide plank with a smoothing plane. Toshio Ōdate is the craftsman demonstrating the techniques.

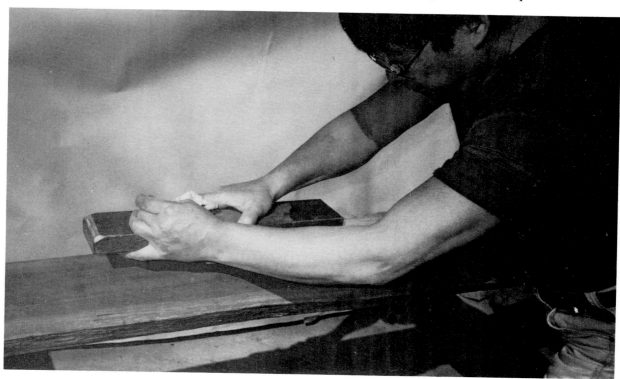

Fig. 82. Edge planing a narrow board using a jointer plane (note that the small finger acts as a fence to assist in guiding the plane): Begin the pass with your arms fully extended.

Fig. 83. Edge planing a narrow board using a jointer plane: Mid-position of pass, with wood-shaving curls showing in plane mouth.

Fig. 84. Edge planing a narrow board using a jointer plane: ¾ position of pass viewed from above, with arms nearing body.

Fig. 85. Edge planing a narrow board with a jointer plane: End of pass; arms close to body.

Fig. 86. Foot position during planing: Begin the pass with weight on the front foot.

Fig. 87. Foot position during planing: At mid-position of pass, weight should be on both feet.

Fig. 88. Foot position during planing: At end of pass, body weight should be transferred to your rear foot.

Fig. 89. Hand positions during the planing of a wide plank using a smoothing plane: At the beginning of the pass, extend arms.

Fig. 90. Hand positions during the planing of a wide plank: Mid-point of pass.

Fig. 91. Hand positions during the planing of a wide plank: Finish of pass; arms close to body.

Maintaining the Blade

To retain a keen cutting edge, that blade must be removed and rehoned every few hours. As each blade and block are fitted as a unit, it is usually not possible to just replace one blade with another. After repeated sharpenings, the flat on the underside of the cutting bevel between the cutting edge and the hollow will become too narrow to seat the chip breaker correctly. See Fig. 92.

To renew this flat to its original width, the soft steel on the cutting bevel must be hammered down to eliminate the hollow in this area. This can be done in a number of ways. Traditionally, it is done by holding the edge of the blade against a firmly supported anvil or a hardwood block and, with a series of carefully directed hammer blows, deforming the blade to fill the hollow. See Fig. 93.

Fig. 92. The underside of a blade with the flat ground away from repeated sharpenings.

Fig. 93. Using a hammer to strike the blade bevel. Note that the cast-iron support absorbing the force of the blow is directly beneath the hammer face.

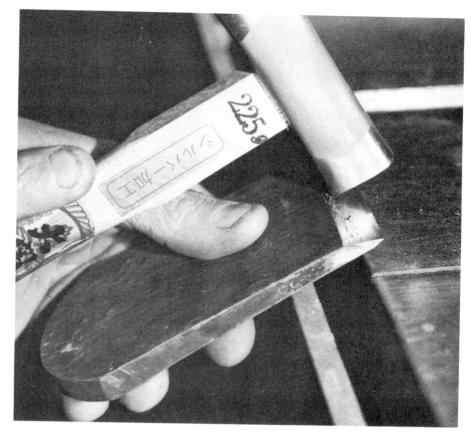

Great care is required so as not to strike the exposed hardened steel laminate of the cutting bevel or to strike any portion with such force that the hard steel layer will be cracked. Ideally, when finished the cutting bevel will show a series of hammer marks across the face similar to those shown in Fig. 94. The farther back from the exposed, hardened steel layer, the thicker the soft-steel layer of the cutting bevel and the greater distance the hollow grind beneath must be hammered out. As the soft steel absorbs some of the shock of the hammer blow, the thicker section can, and must be, struck with a greater force.

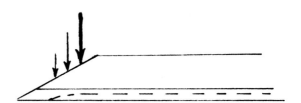

Fig. 94. Note the pattern of impact marks that occur when you hammer down the blade. The wider dashes and darker arrows indicate a harder striking force.

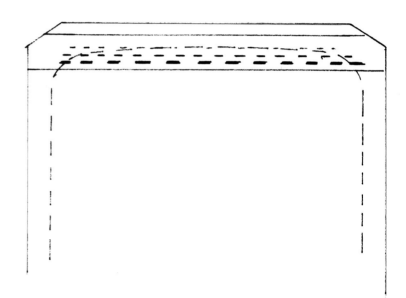

A safer method for someone who has trouble directing a hammer blow with any precision is to clamp the blade tightly to a flat anvil and hammer down the cutting bevel using the rounded corner of a firmly held pin punch that is at least ½ inch (12.7 mm) in diameter. See Fig. 95. A mechanical means of performing this technique is provided by a tool which clamps the blade against an anvil and uses a guided plunger as a hammer force. See Figs. 96 and 97.

After a flat has been reestablished, the back of the blade must be reground. As it will have considerable roughness at this point, it will be necessary to start the flattening process using a coarse-grit silicon carbide and a soft-steel lapping plate as described on pages 62 and 63.

Today flat, laminated plane blades are being made in Japan to fit Western metal planes. While there is great resistance on the part of traditionalists, this same concept is appearing on some tapered blades being made without a hollow grind on the back to fit Japanese planes. The prime difficulty is in being able to lap the entire back flat, in contrast to only a narrow band around the edges. This can easily be done on production grinding and lapping equipment. In theory, blades from identical steels should perform equally with or without a hollow grind on the back when these backs are given equal flatness and smoothness.

Fig. 95. Using a pin punch to strike the soft iron of the cutting bevel. This method permits greater accuracy in directing the impact of the blow.

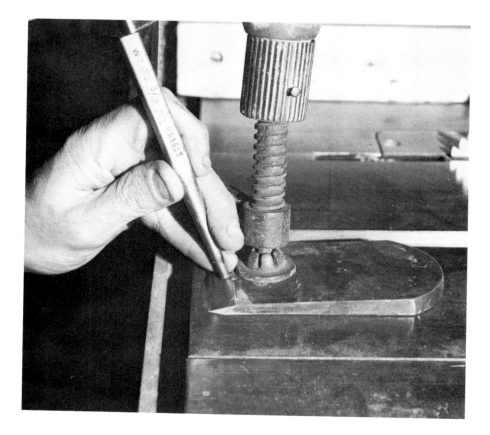

Fig. 96. Using a mechanical blade flattener will positively control the accuracy of the impact.

Fig. 97. A closeup look at the mechanical blade flattener. The lines drawn on the soft-steel portion of the cutting bevel indicate striking planes.

Fig. 98. Here the blade flattening has been finished and the blade is ready to be resurfaced and ground. As all of the impact marks are on the soft-steel portion of the cutting bevel, they are quickly ground away.

Specialty Planes

Looking through the catalogue of today's Japanese specialty plane makers is like reading a description of the planes used by a finishing carpenter, stairbuilder or other craftsmen of a century ago. They could have a tool box containing as many as 100 moulding planes to produce the profiles needed to make their end product. Included might be shapes for hollows and rounds and tongues and grooves in various widths, door- and window-frame profiles, sliding dovetails, mouldings, and cornices, in addition to the more prosaic dado and rabbet planes.

Fig. 99. These finger planes are 2 to 3″ (5.1 to 7.6 cm) long. Top row, from left to right, they are: 1 & 2, smoothing planes; 3 & 4, convex end to end; 5–6, convex end to end and side to side (spoon bottom); 7 & 8, concave end to end and side to side; 9–11, hollowing; 12–14, rounding. Bottom row from left to right, they are: 1 & 2, rabbetting; 3, V-Groove; 4 & 5, r and l corner rabbet planes; 6, chamfering inside corner; 7 & 8, r and l side rabbet.

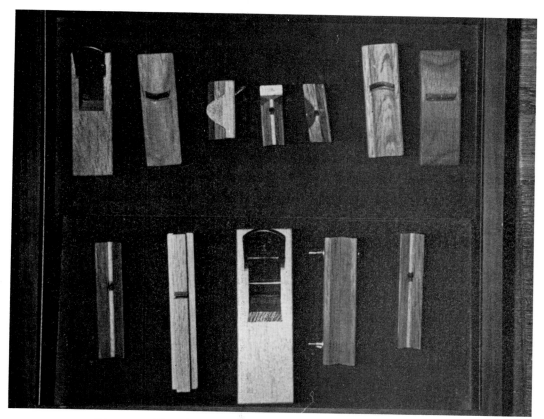

*Fig. 100. Here is a set of small cabinetmaker's planes. The longest is 5"
(12.7 cm). Top row from left to right, they are: block plane, hollowing plane,
r, l, and straight rounding planes, rounding plane, and compass plane. On
the bottom row, from left to right, are: beading plane, dado plane with depth
stop, smoothing plane, adjustable chamfer plane, and a beading plane. Figs. 99
and 100 were taken on the floor of the factory office in Sanjo, Japan, by the
author. The boxes are resting on a patterned* tatami *mat floor.*

Some of these can still be found in the catalogue of the firm
of Lachappelle of Switzerland.

The moulding planes so widely used in earlier times were
supplanted by the Stanley 45 and 55 and the Record Multi-
plane, which combined in one plane as many as 93 different
profiles for dadoes, beads, sash cutting, stair nosing, hollow
and rounding, etc. These planes also had depth stops and side
fences to control the size of cuts, as well as forecutters to score
the wood in advance of the main cutting blade. These planes
in turn have largely given way to the shaper and router.

Most of these single-purpose specialty planes are still available in Japan in some form today. Commonly seen are side rabbet planes, edge-trimming planes, fillister and dovetail planes, hollowing and rounding planes and planes with two separate main irons to cut a wide complex profile. This type of double-iron plane was made in England as early as the 18th century to make cornice mouldings. Separating the profile into two pieces makes it easier to form and to sharpen. It also makes the plane block much stronger by eliminating the need to cut the plane mouth and throat to the full width of the profile being cut. See Fig. 101.

There are several specialty moulding planes that are very useful even today. One is the adjustable chamfering plane which cuts accurate chamfers to 1 inch (2.5 cm) wide. Rules are embedded in the front and back of the main block for setting the desired chamfer width, which is then locked with a pair of knurled nuts. The blade is held in a separate removeable body which allows easy blade fitting and setting. A small "pocket" version of this plane only 3 inches (7.6 cm) long which will cut a ½-inch (12.7-mm)-wide chamfer is also made. Fig. 104 shows both planes.

Fig. 101. The side rebate plane only cuts on its side.

Fig.102. Dovetail plane with forecutters.

Fig. 103. A cornice plane with two separate irons to cut a complete profile.

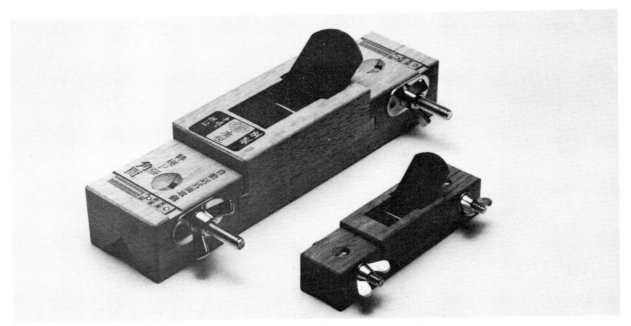

Fig. 104. Two adjustable chamfering planes. The smaller is 3″ (7.6 cm)
long.

Fig. 105. The adjustable
chamfering plane being
used to chamfer an edge.

Another useful plane is the beading plane which can have a fixed shoulder depth or, in a variation, is fitted with adjustable side fences to permit shoulders of varying depths on either side. Many different profiles are available in a range of widths. For some of the possible forms, see Fig. 108. These planes are sometimes made with the blade skewed at an angle to the plane block, so that when cutting across the wood fibres it produces a slicing action which reduces the possibility of grain tear-out.

Fig. 106. A beading plane with adjustable shoulders (viewed from the bottom).

Fig. 107. A beading plane used to cut a corner profile.

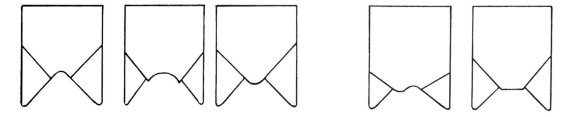

Fig. 108. Some of the possible beading plane profiles available.

IV · CHISELS

While much of the chisel production of Japan today is of the plastic-handled, drop-forged blade design made the world over, the discussion here will be confined to the traditional design with laminated blade and hooped wooden handle. This design permits the use of an extremely hard steel laminate for the cutting edge, and the use of a steel-faced striking hammer for maximum force.

The process of forging a steel insert to an iron blade is not unique to Japan. It was frequently used by the American blacksmith in the 19th century, and was used on production plane irons and chisels in Europe. This was a way to save scarce, valuable steel when making the tool, and also a way to replace a wearing surface without making an entirely new tool. With only a small portion of the cutting bevel hardened steel, it is also easier to resharpen the cutting edge.

The Japanese chisel-making process consists of the joining of a soft iron or steel body to a steel cutting edge that can be hardened. While in the past this has been done by hammer-forged welding at 1000 °C, it is now in some instances being done by roll forging two billets of steel together at the mill. This gives a far more precise control over the laminating process, and also permits the use of tougher alloy steels or even high-speed steels for the cutting edge. This mill process is a significant improvement because it can be done at a lower temperature without decarburizing the steel. As a result, the heat-treating process used to obtain final edge hardening is much easier to control.

The laminated blank is reheated to 900–950 °C, and the shank and tang hot-forged on the soft steel end. Next, the

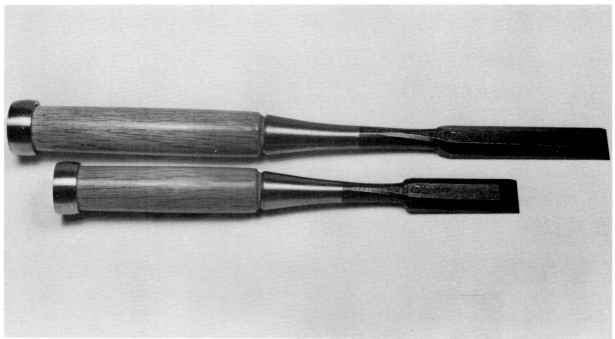

Fig. 109. Closeup of chisels.

Fig. 110. Parts of the chisel from lower right to upper left: blade with forged neck and tang, steel socket, wood handle and steel hoop.

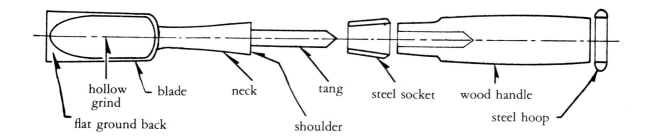

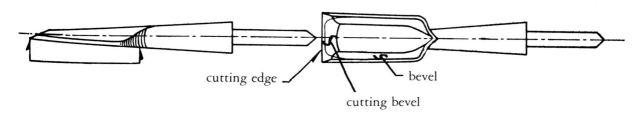

Fig. 111. Diagam showing illustrated parts of the chisel.

Fig. 112. Handle turned from boxwood blank.

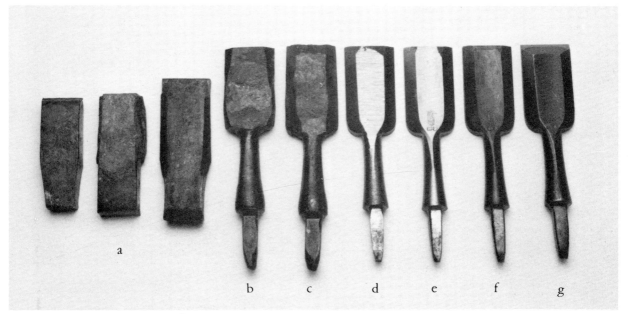

Fig. 113. A: initial steps in forging and laminating of carbon-steel blank to soft steel body; b; forging the shank and tang; c, annealed forging; d, rough grinding; e, finish grinding; f, hardened and tempered; g, finished blade.

Fig. 114. This forging blank for chisel blades shows hard and soft layers before lamination and when the blade is finished.

blade will be sized in a forging press at 850–900 °C, which is followed by an annealing to relieve forging stresses. It will then be straightened, ground to shape, hardened, tempered and given a final straightening. This is followed by hollow grinding of the back, final forming and polishing, after which the finished tool is handled.

Unlike a Western socket chisel, in which the socket is formed by piercing the shank of the blade, the socket on the Japanese chisel is a separately formed piece. It is assembled to the chisel at the time the handle is driven onto the tang. As the blade shank and this bottom socket ring are then ground as a unit, a fine circumferential line, which is sometimes mistaken for an apparent defect in the shank, appears at this juncture point between the socket ring and the chisel shoulder. Fig. 112 shows the steps in the blade-forging process.

The hollow-ground relief on the back of the blade that is a characteristic of the Japanese chisel is found in two different configurations: a single full-width relief regardless of width, or a multiple set of grooves whose number depends upon the width of the blade. Figs. 115 and 116 show single and multi-groove sets.

The hollow grind apparently was introduced to reduce the amount of material on the back of the chisel that had to be removed to make the back completely flat for use. With the soft, fast-wearing Japanese waterstone, it would result in a great saving of valuable natural sharpening stone. The multiple relief design provides additional flat lands for support when using the chisel at an angle near the edge of the workpiece. It also provides additional control to prevent a chisel from digging in when sizing deep mortises.

Recent tests have indicated that for chisels up to 1 inch (2.5 cm) in width there is no significant difference in the flattening of an unrelieved chisel or a hollow-ground chisel when using a synthetic waterstone. This design eliminates the necessity of regrinding the chisel back to reposition the relief as the cutting edge is ground back during resharpenings.

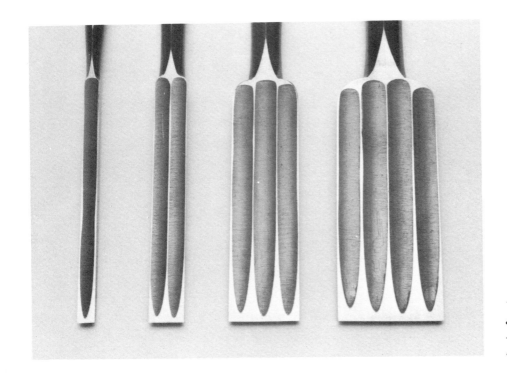

Fig. 115. Hollow-
ground backs of chisels
showing multiple-groove
hollow designs.

Fig. 116. Hollow-
ground backs showing
full-width hollow.

Number of grooves vs. width of chisels
with multiple groove backs

Width of Chisel	No. of Grooves
3–9 mm	1
12–24 mm	2
24–48 mm	3
42–54 mm	4

There is no industry standard, so the table shows
an overlap found while checking various maker's chisels.

Fig. 117. Table showing width of chisels vs. number of grooves.

Conditioning a Chisel for Use

Before a striking chisel can be used for the first time, the steel hoop at the top end of the handle must be seated to ensure that it will remain in place and also that in use the hammer actually strikes a cushion of wood and not the steel hoop.

As a result of the wood drying and shrinking, the top ring on a new chisel will usually not stay in place. To seat the ring properly, it must be removed and the handle lightly swaged. This can be done by holding the upper end of the handle on an anvil and tapping it firmly with a steel hammer until the ring just seats about $\frac{1}{32}$ to $\frac{1}{16}$ inch below the top of the handle. The compacted wood will naturally expand to lock the ring in place. This effect can be hastened by just dipping the top of the handle in water. In reseating the ring, note that it is probably not symmetrical on the inside but has a wider taper on its lower end which eases its replacement on the handle.

Through use, the wood that projects above the ring will mushroom over slightly to form a cushion for the hammer blow. A more symmetrical crown can be started by initially hammering around the top edge of the handle.

In a new chisel sometimes the gap between the socket and the overhanging shoulder on the wooden handle is too narrow. If this shoulder bears on the socket, all the driving force of the hammer blow is transmitted through the relatively thin walls of the socket, and it may buckle. (The main function of this lower ring is to keep the wood handle from splitting away from the tang.) To widen this gap remove the handle from the chisel blade before trimming back the shoulder. To remove the handle, hold the chisel upside down by the blade and rap the handle against a solid vertical surface. After several blows the handle should slide from the chisel tang. As the

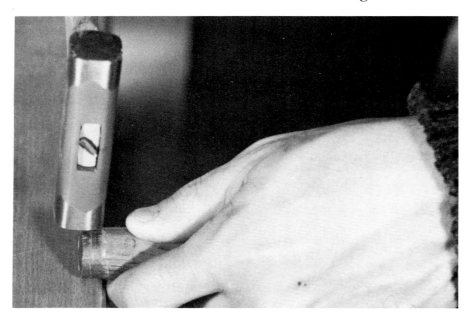

Fig. 118. Swaging the upper end of the chisel handle to compact the wood for proper seating of the steel ring.

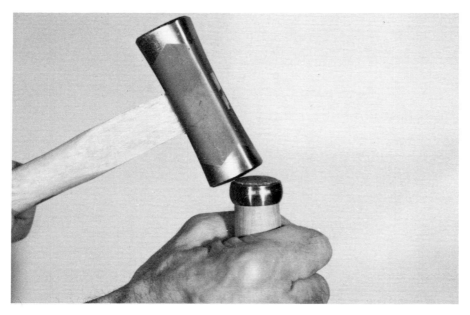

Fig. 119. Forming the mushroom cap to retain the ring in position and to cushion the force of the hammer blow.

socket and tang shoulder are machined as a unit after assembly, it is a good idea to put match marks on the mating pieces before removing the handle.

By tradition many chisels sold in Japan are not finish-ground on the cutting bevel or at the joint between the shank and the socket. The user is expected to sharpen the tool to his liking.

Types of Chisels

As the traditional chisel makers have small shops with hand-controlled forging and grinding operations, small quantities can be economically made. This means that an infinite number of variations are possible. In Japan, the most commonly used chisel is the butt chisel. The blade length is about 2½ inches (6.4 cm) and widths range from ⅟₁₆ to 2½ inches (1.5 to 6.4 cm). A longer blade length of about 7 inches (17.8 cm) that is more familiar to the Western woodworker is also made in the same widths. In addition, a framing chisel with a blade section about 40 percent heavier is also made in widths to 2 inches (5.1 cm). These are all bevel-edge chisels but because of the forging process blades under ½ inches (12.7 mm) are normally straight-sided without a bevelled edge. The cutting bevel is usually sharpened to a 26°–28° cutting angle. Since the cutting edge has been hardened to R_c63 or higher, it must be used only for cutting and not to pry out partially cut pieces of wood. Any attempt to pry may well break out a piece of the cutting edge. The same problem can also occur if the chisel is not held firmly while being struck, but is allowed to waver when advancing into the wood.

The mortise chisel is a short-blade, heavy-section chisel made in widths to ¾ inches (19.0 cm). It has a steeper cutting bevel angle of 35° to take the stresses of prying wood from a mortise as it is being cut.

After a joint has been sawed to shape, it is often pared to final size with a slick or dovetail chisel fitted with a longer un-hooped handle designed only to be pushed and not struck. The cutting edge on these paring chisels is 24°. For large joinery, a slick can have a blade 2½ inches (6.4 cm) wide and a 15-inch (38.1-cm)-long handle.

While the corner dovetail so common to Western joinery is not normally seen in traditional Japanese cabinetry, the sliding dovetail is frequently encountered. To cut this joint, there are push chisels with triangular cross sections and narrow shoulders to clean narrow grooves or long dovetails. They are available with a straight or a dogleg blade in widths from ¼ to 1½ inch (6.4 to 38.1 mm).

To satisfy the needs of the Western craftsman who prefers the Japanese chisel construction, a striking dovetail chisel has been developed. The triangular section has a narrow or even zero bevel shoulder, and a base angle as low as 15° in the larger sizes. The shank is bent so that the handle clears the surface of the workpiece when paring.

In addition to the more common styles of chisels, there are chisels developed for specialized crafts and joinery. A very useful set are used for cutting and clearing the small mortises that are found in *shoji,* the sliding screen found in all tradi-

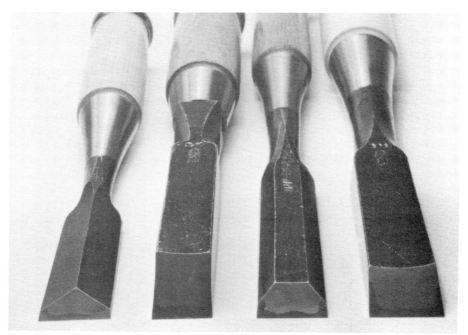

Fig. 120. From left to right: dovetail chisel, mortise chisel, bevel-edge chisel, and heavy-duty firmer chisel.

tional Japanese houses. The straight chisel has a hooked tip used to remove chips from the mortise. It is driven into the waste and pulled up to clear out the chip. The curved shank chisel has a tip shaped like an adze and is used to scrape the bottom of the mortise flat. To clean the corners of the mortise, there is a sickle-shaped chisel which acts as a knife to score the corner.

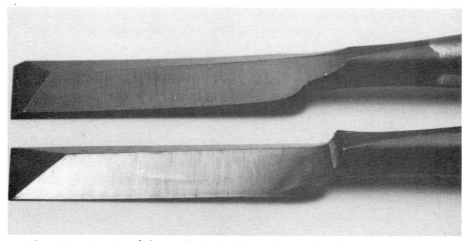

Fig. 121. A pair of dovetail chisels: The chisel in the foreground has no side shoulders.

Fig. 122. Mortise chisel.

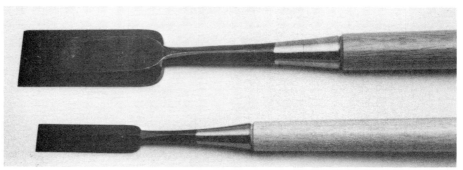

Fig. 123. Slick (top) and paring chisel (bottom).

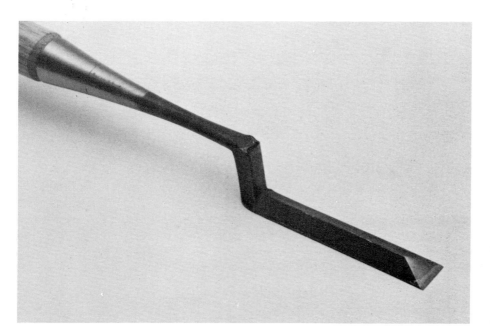

Fig.124. Dogleg chisel (offset paring chisel).

Fig. 125. Paring cross grain with an offset paring chisel.

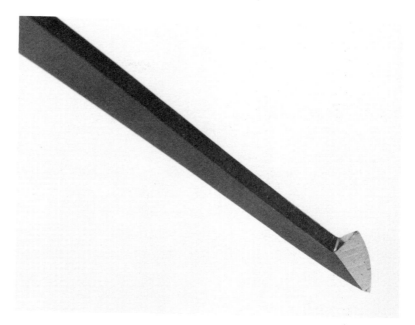

Fig 126. Sickle-shaped chisel.

Fig. 127. A pair of chisels used in cutting small mortises.

For large mortises, an actual corner chisel with 90° corners is made to pare a right angle. The corner chisel can be particularly difficult to use as any attempt to pry out a cut chip can fracture the cutting edge. It cannot be used as a conventional mortise chisel as it has a much lower cutting bevel angle.

A chisel buyer cannot tell by looking at a tool what its cutting-edge quality is. It may be made from high-carbon or high-speed steel or even carbide. Rockwell hardness for the various steels would normally be: high carbon, R_c63; HSS or alloy steel, R_c65; tool steel, R_c67. The softer body can be hot-rolled, low-carbon steel or a special wrought iron salvaged from old anchor chain and bridges. This particular material was especially important in the past, as the glasslike slag impurities present would scour the surface of a stone used to sharpen the cutting bevel and renew its cutting action. This scouring action is of value only with certain natural stones.

Chisel handles may be of red or white oak, boxwood, sandalwood, ebony, or even sharkskin covered. Red oak is the most popular, though white oak is somewhat stronger. Boxwood has a springy property that absorbs some of the shock of the hammer blow. While this reduces the cutting force somewhat, it is also easier on the hand of the user.

An expensive chisel is not necessarily better than a moderately priced chisel. The high cost can result from the special workmanship needed to produce a decorative pattern in the soft-iron body, rare woods in the handle, and hand-forged hoops. These chisels can be a work of art and a joy to behold, in addition to being simply utilitarian. For examples of two such chisels, see Figs. 129 and 130. These were made by Mr. Iyoroi of Miki City, who is one of the most progressive chisel makers in Japan today.

Various furniture carving gouges are shown on page 108.

Fig. 128. Corner chisel.

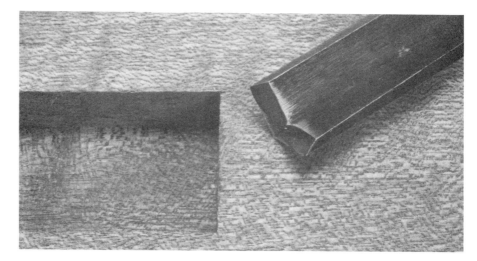

Fig. 129. Note the multiple lamination on the soft iron of this chisel. This chisel was made by Iyoroi, of Miki City.

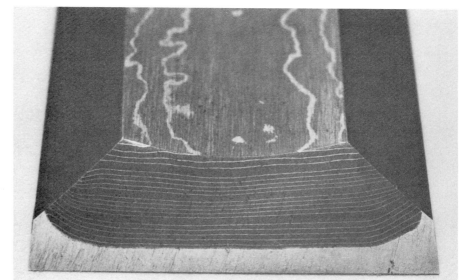

Fig. 130. The etched and twisted soft iron on this chisel reveals inclusions and flow patterns in the wrought iron. This chisel was also made by Iyoroi of Miki City.

Fig. 131. Gouge for fur-niture carving: Dia-mond-point gouge.

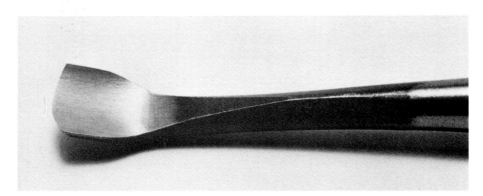

Fig. 132. Gouge for fur-niture carving: Bent gouge.

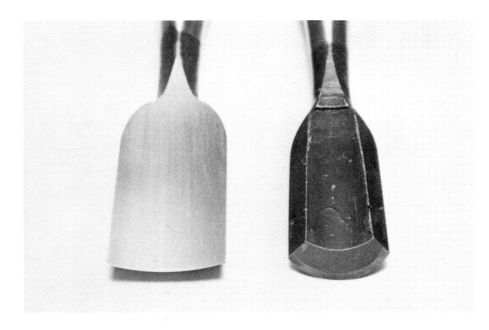

Fig. 133. Gouges for furniture carving: At left, firmer gouge. At right, incannel gouge.

Fig. 141. Sharpening a chisel: Continue sharpening the chisel on a whetstone grinder.

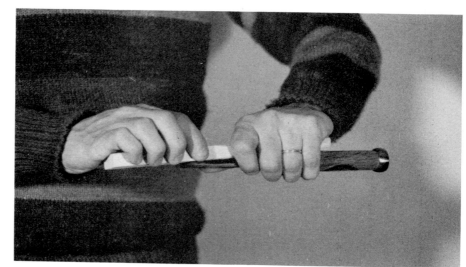

Fig. 142. Sharpening a chisel: Use a wooden pressure bar to flatten the back. This technique is especially useful when it becomes necessary to widen the flat under the cutting edge.

Fig. 143. Using a wooden pressure bar to flatten the back.

Fig. 144. Using a strik-ing chisel with a steel hammer.

Fig. 145. Bevel edge.

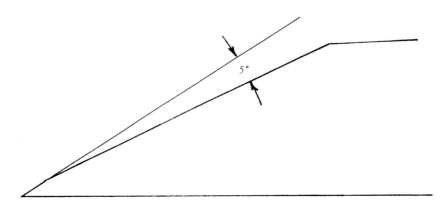

V · MEASURING AND MARKING TOOLS

Framing Squares

Unlike the heavy, broad, flat arms of the Western square, the traditional Japanese equivalent has a flexible, thin narrow arm with shaped profile. When used for measuring, the blade is laid on the bevelled face so that the scale graduations almost touch the surface being measured. This minimizes parallax (see Glossary, page 150) and allows a very accurate measurement. When an arm is used as a guide for ruling with a knife or pen, it provides a space between the guiding edge and the workpiece. When it is used with a knife, this means that the knife blade has less chance to cut into the square as the sharpened cutting edge is beneath the guiding edge. When it is used with a pen, it means that the chance of ink being drawn under the edge by capillary attraction (see Glossary, page 149) is eliminated. Even with a pencil, it eliminates the annoying graphite dust so often produced by drawing the pencil point along the incised scale graduations.

These squares are now made from a rolled section of hardened stainless steel welded to a softer right-angle corner piece. The softer and thicker corner piece permits the square to be adjusted for angular accuracy. As with Western squares, it is possible to close the angle in by hitting outside the centerline of the corner diagonal with a center punch or by striking the inside to open the angle. The punch locally spreads the metal, which widens that particular spot.

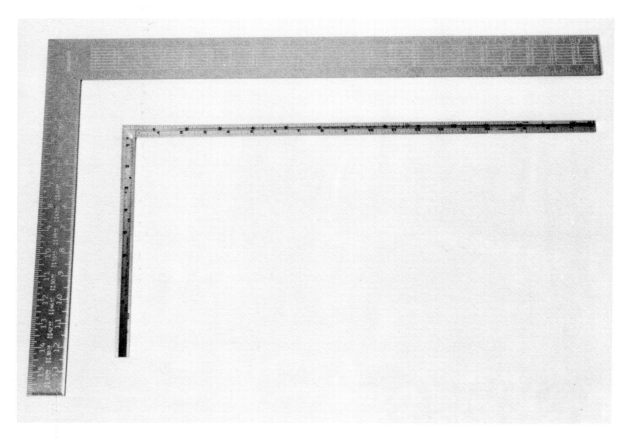

Fig. 146. Profile of a framing square. (Illustration is approximately three times the size of the profile.)

Fig. 147. Framing squares. The one on top is a Western framing square with rafter tables. The other one is a Japanese framing square with circumference and diagonal scales.

Fig. 148. Squaring a board with a framing square. The framing square's flexibility allows it to be held tightly to the workpiece.

Fig. 149.   Scoring a mark with a square and knife.

Japanese squares were traditionally marked in a measuring system based on divisions of the *shaku,* which is about one foot in length. For many years, they have been made with metric markings, and more recently have been introduced with inch graduations. In addition to the standard inside and out-side scales, they have two unusual scales on the underside. The outer scale on the long leg is called *kakume* and is actually the standard scale multiplied by 1.414 or the square root of 2. This means that the 1-inch (2.5-cm) graduation actually mea-sures 1.414 inches and results in a reading which is the length of the side of a square if the scale is laid across the diagonal of that square. See Fig. 152. Its purpose is to determine the size of a square beam which can be cut from a round log.

On the inner face of the short leg is the *marume* scale, which is the result of multiplying the standard scale by 2 pi or 6.2832. Using this to measure the width of a circle or round log will actually give a reading equal to the circumference. See Fig. 153. On the end of the long leg following the *kakume* scale is a 3-inch (7.6-cm) vertical scale reading up from the end which can be used to measure the depth of a hole or mor-tise or the length of a tenon. See Fig. 151.

Fig. 150. Closeup of scales on the Japanese framing square. (Note the formu-lae and diagrams etched on the scales for Figs. 152 to 154.) The corner sec-tion of the scale has a thicker welded corner insert.

Fig. 151. Note the depth-measuring scale on the end of the long leg of the framing square.

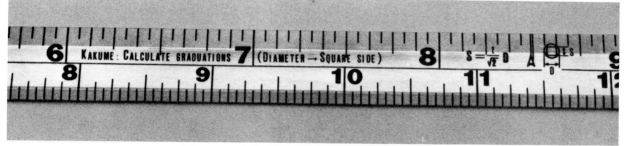

Fig. 152. The diagonal or diameter scale, which determines the length of the sides of the enclosing scale, is the outer scale on the long leg.

Fig. 153. The diameter scale, which is on the inner face of the short leg, determines the circumference of the enclosing circle.

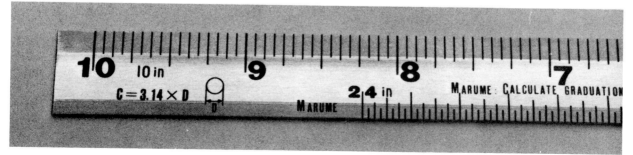

Fig. 154. Continuation of diagonal scale.

Mitre Squares

As a guide for sawing, the Japanese craftsman may use a wooden gauge as a fence to guide the blade in starting a cut. While they are usually sold to serve as a guide to cut a 45° mitre, they can easily be made for any desired single or compound angle. See Fig. 156. These saw guides have evolved into more permanent metal marking gauges. An added feature found on some of the newer models is a graduated scale on the 45° mitre face which is similar to the *kakume* scale in concept in that the measurement reading is the actual vertical distance from the edge of the workpiece.

Fig. 155. Wooden mitre square.

Fig. 156. Wooden mitre square used as a saw fence.

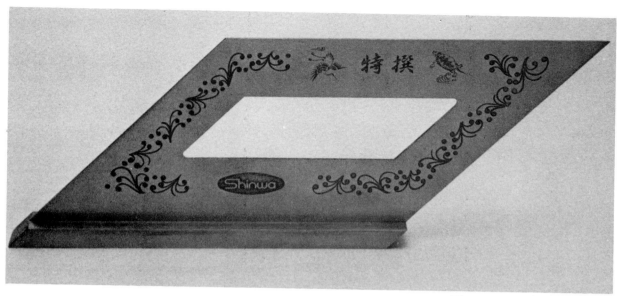

Fig. 157. Steel mitre square.

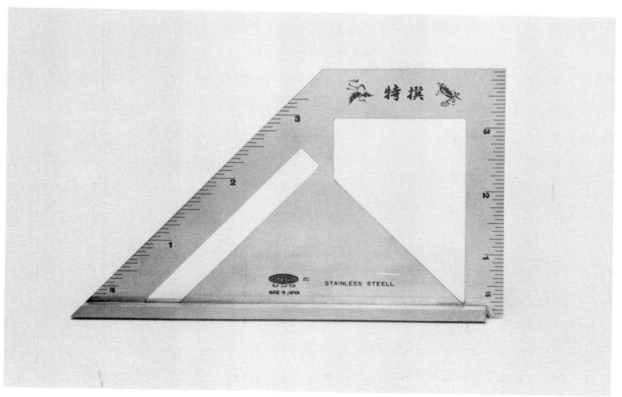

Fig. 158. Graduated mitre square.

Marking Gauges

Most Japanese marking gauges made today are variations of cutting gauges with one or two stems or blades locked in a fence by a thumbscrew. They are made in many patterns and sizes primarily from red or white oak. To reduce wear on the face they may have an ebony insert or, for decorative effect, be made entirely of ebony or other tropical hardwood.

The basic cutting gauge has a fixed knife in a moveable beam. The more complex mortise/marking gauge has two forms: moveable double beams with fixed blades and fixed beams with two moveable steel-cutting arms. Blades are always

Fig. 159. Marking gauges: At top, a gauge with a single moveable beam; at bottom left, a gauge with two moveable beams; at bottom right, a gauge with two moveable blades.

bevelled on one side only and when used as a mortise gauge the bevelled sides of the cutting edges face each other so that they are on the inside of the lines being scribed. See Fig. 160. When used as a cutting gauge, the unused blade on a moveable blade gauge is retracted into a recess in the fence. On a double-beam gauge, the unused beam can be reversed so that its knife is behind the fence. Figs. 160 to 164 show how to use a marking guage.

Fig. 160. Using the marking gauge: These two moveable beams have been extended to lay out a dado.

Fig. 161. Here, one beam has been reversed to be used as a cutting gauge.

Fig. 162. In this marking gauge, two moveable blades have been extended to lay out a dado.

Fig. 163. Here, the moveable blade has been retracted so the tool can be used as a cutting gauge.

Fig. 164. Single-beam cutting gauge.

Marking And Woodworking Knives

The single-bevel marking knife for use with squares and straightedges is made in both right- and left-hand versions. While possibly not as practical, these marking knives are also made in the shape of a fish or other objects. The large "fish"-shaped version depicted in Fig. 165 was hand-forged by Mr. Iyoroi.

Whether for trimming, paring or carving, there are many shapes and sizes of laminated blade knives. Some are bare blades such as the marking knives. Some have bamboo-wrapped handles, while others have wooden handles or wooden handles plus a protective wooden blade sheath. Some of the various forms are depicted in Fig. 166.

When the blade of the knife is enclosed in a wooden sheath, it is possible to determine the position of the cutting edge within by observing the cut-off corner at one end of the sheath. The sharpened side of the knife end will face the spot. To open, hold the case with one hand grasping each side and the notched corner facing front. With the thumb of the hand holding the notched side, push on the other half of the case to slide off the blade sheath about ¼-inch (6.4-mm). Then pull both hands straight apart to remove the knife blade from its sheath.

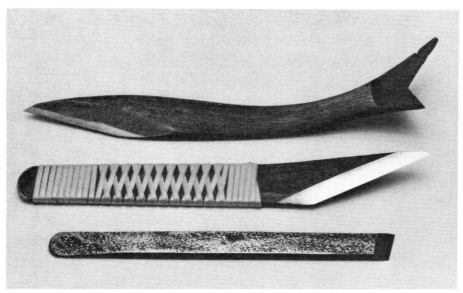

Fig. 165. Marking knives.

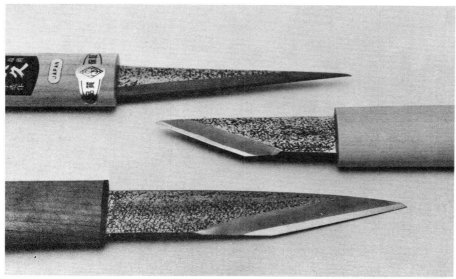

Fig. 166. Woodworking knives.

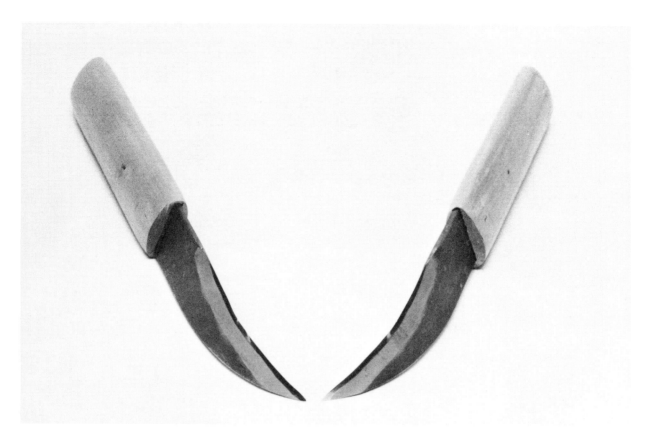

Fig. 167. Right- and left-hand curved blade knives. These are useful for bowl carving.

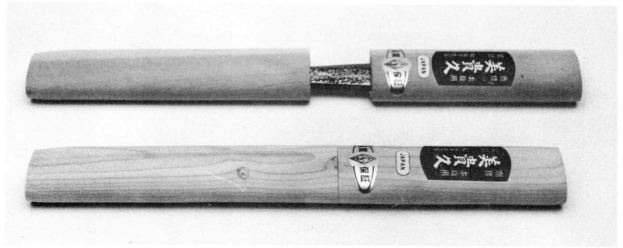

Fig. 168. Sheath knives closed and partially opened. Note the notch in the upper left-hand corner which designates the sharpened side and tip of the blade.

VI · MISCELLANEOUS TOOLS

Gimlets

Some common Japanese tools, such as the bit and brace, are similar to their Western counterparts. Others such as gimlets, which are used for drilling small diameter holes for starting screws—especially in soft wood—differ in their design concepts. To use the Japanese gimlet, spin the round, tapered handle between your hands while exerting enough downward pressure to force the point into the wood, yet not so much pressure as to cause it to bind or, with the forked-tip version, break off a point.

Hammers

Hammers are available in a wide variety of shapes, weights and styles depending upon their intended use and also the skills of the craftsman who did the forging. Heads can be made either from a solid, drop-forged billet or with the more traditional soft body with laminated hard-steel faces. The production method probably depends upon limitations of equipment available, as only the larger shops would have the large presses required to make a drop-forged head. There is no advantage to the laminated construction; the soft-iron core, in comparison to the thin wooden handle, is not better able to "dampen out" the vibration impact of the hard steel. With either construction, the faces of the carpenter's hammer would be hardened; one would be ground flat and the other slightly convex.

Fig. 169. Three shapes of gimlet heads.

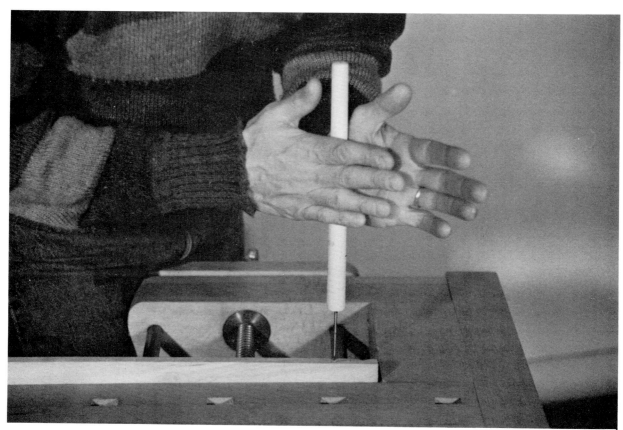

Fig. 170. Use the gimlet by spinning it between the palms of both hands.

Fig. 171. Laminated head hammers with differing cross sections.

Fig. 172. Closeup of a laminated square-head hammer.

Fig. 173. Forged heads with embossed and engraved tiger and dragon designs.

Hatchets

Hatchets are made in two distinct forms. One is the basic axe shape with the wooden handle at right angles to the head. The head will usually be modified in form, as shown in Fig. 174, for stylistic reasons in addition to giving a more efficient weight distribution. The cutting edge is a hardened steel piece which has been cast forged into the overlapping soft-steel head. The second form is similar to a short, heavy-bladed machete with a handle in line with the blade. This design is usually easier for the unskilled to control. Blade lengths vary from 6 to 9 inches (15.2 to 22.9 cm) and some forms have chisel tips at the end of the blade. When not in use, the blade is usually protected by a wooden sheath. The blade has a single cutting bevel with the hardened steel lamination on the flat side.

Fig. 174. Two carpenter's hatchets.

Fig. 175. "Machete"-style hatchets. The smaller hatchet has a chisel tip.

Nail Puller

Another useful tool is a nail puller, sometimes known as a cat's paw. It is made in lengths from 7 to 30 inches (17.8 to 76.2 cm). Each length will fit only a limited range of nail sizes in its claws, so that a range of sizes is required for most efficient use. As the claw has only a slight curvature, it is possible to drive the claw under a nailhead without damaging the wood surrounding the nail. The flat on the back of the claw is designed so that it can be struck to drive the horizontal claw under the nailhead. Because of the moderate curvature on the claw, however, the nail cannot be completely levered out without first putting a block under the claw for added leverage.

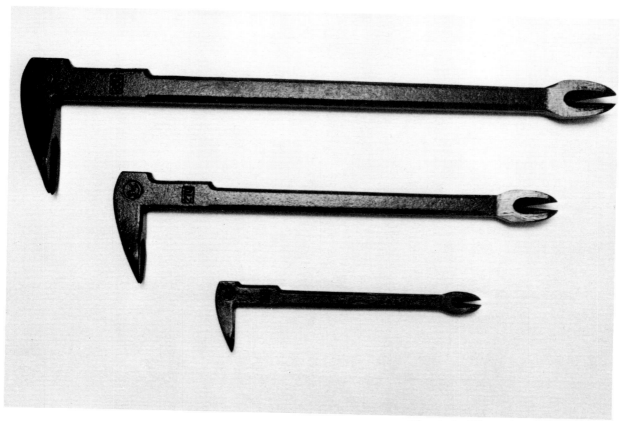

Fig. 176. Three sizes of nail pullers.

Fig. 177. Closeup of nail puller heads.

Fig. 178. Using a nail puller: Drive the claw under the nail head.

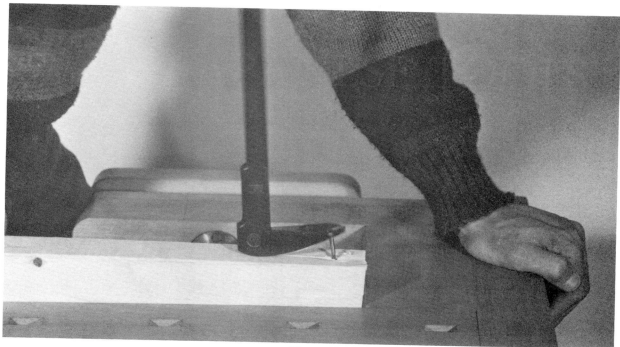

Fig. 179. Using a nail puller: Start to lever out the nail.

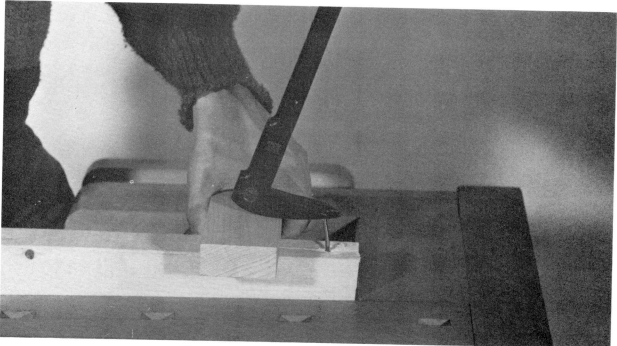

Fig. 180. Using a nail puller: Remove the nail by using the aid of the block under the claw to increase leverage.

Clamps

Japanese gluing clamps are light in weight and fast to position for holding. Clamps from 3 to 12 inches (7.6 to 30.5 cm) in length are usually made of brass while those from 12 inches and up are made of steel. The clamp is set to the work by sliding the tail stop on the beam and locking it to length with a toggle or thumbscrew. Clamping pressure is then applied by closing in the opposing face on the head of the clamp with a screw that bears directly on the back of the clamping jaw. One disadvantage, however, is that the short depth of the clamp jaw and the small size of the clamping screw limit the clamping pressure that may be applied.

Fig. 181.   Gluing clamp showing details of head and stop.

Fig. 182. Using a clamp for gluing.

Camellia Oil

Japanese craftsmen have used camellia oil as a rust preventative in the same fashion as aerosol spray oils are used in Western workshops. It is a natural oil made from the camellia plant. Any residue left on the hands after using it on tools not only smells better than the typical penetrating oil, but is probably beneficial as well.

Since most Japanese tools are made from carbon steel, it is important that they occasionally receive a light coating of a nonstaining oil. This is especially true after sharpening edge tools on a waterstone where water has replaced the oil normally used with Western sharpening stones. A few moments spent drying off the tool and wiping on a light film of oil can prevent the formation of rust, which not only creates a poor impression but also makes it difficult, if not impossible, to produce a keen edge on a cutting tool.

Fig. 183. Camellia oil.

VII · UNUSUAL JAPANESE TOOLS

The tools shown in the preceding chapters all have great appeal to the average woodworker. Included in this section are some tools that might have little practical value to woodworkers, but are intriguing nonetheless.

The *sumitsubo* is the traditional Japanese equivalent to the chalk line and plumb line. It has changed little over the years and can be seen in many of the old prints showing carpenters at work. See the prints on pages 14 and 140. In use, as a chalk line, the silk line is unwound from the reel and passes through an ink-filled wadding. A pin fastened to the end of the line holds it in place as the line is stretched over the workpiece. By locking the reel and hanging the case from the pin, it can be used as a plumb line. The *sumitsubo* pictured on page 141 would retail for about $30. However, they can be very ornately carved and the most elaborate oversized models used for ceremonial programs can cost as much as $2,000.

One of the workmen on page 14 is using a bamboo marking stick. Since bamboo is a very fibrous material, a brush can be formed by crushing the end on an anvil with light hammer blows. The resulting brush can be dipped in ink and used for marking and layout work on timbers. The stick can also be used to compress the wadding in the *sumitsubo* to ensure a thorough wetting of the silk line as it is drawn through the ink-filled wadding.

Fig. 184. Wood block print of carpenters at work.

Fig. 185. Sumitsubo *and bamboo marking stick.*

The *chona* is the equivalent of the adze and is the tool that was used for the rough squaring of timbers and boards. The curved handle of the *chona* is formed by tying down a suitable sapling while it is growng. After it has been deformed into the proper shape, the sapling is cut down, debarked and fitted to the *chona* head. As with the Western foot adze, the user stands on the timber being shaped and strikes the wood just in front of his foot. Fig. 184 shows a worker in the foreground using a *chona* to hew a beam.

Before the plane was developed, the Japanese carpenter used a *yariganna* or spearhead plane to smooth the adze marks from the hewn board. About the only place that the *yariganna* shape is seen today is in a small version for use in woodcarving. See Fig. 186.

The double-edge dogleg dado chisel (called a *kotinomi*) can be used on either the push or pull stroke. The bottom is bevelled from the center to both cutting edges, so that only the edge being used remains in contact with the workpiece. The blade is secured to the leg by a sliding dovetail, which makes it easy to remove for sharpening or storage.

Another useful chisel is the double blade mortise chisel, which has two separate parallel blades and is used to cut twin mortises simultaneously. Though it is a difficult tool to use properly, it ensures the perfect fit between several pair of mortises with their matching double tenons. This frame construction is used on certain types of Japanese doors. Both blades are about ¼″ wide and the gap between them is also about ¼″.

In Japan today, woodcarvers can often be seen at work restoring the many old temples and also carving heads for dolls or puppets. Older carvers have told me that their apprenticeships lasted as long as nine years. As with most Japanese tools, carving gouges and chisels are made from laminated steel. Figs. 189 to 191 show various carving tool shapes and styles.

Fig. 186. Small version of yarikanna *for use as a scraping tool when carving.*

Fig. 187. Double-edge dogleg dado chisel.

Fig. 188. Double blade mortise chisel.

Fig. 189.   Small push hand carving set.

Fig. 190. Small push handle set with etched steel handles.

Fig. 191. Larger carving set with boxwood striking handles.

Knives, Shears and Saws

In my visits to the various toolmakers in Japan, I have found several items for personal use that I consider especially good. These include laminated-steel kitchen knives which are made of a piece of high-carbon steel sandwiched between outer layers of stainless steel. With this construction, the user has all the benefits of a high-carbon cutting edge without the problems of a blade that quickly stains or rusts.

Another useful household item has been shears formed from a single strip of steel. The smaller versions are about 4 inches (10.2 cm) long and have a multitude of uses: tying flies, removing stitches, cutting ribbon and string, and pruning plants.

Fig. 192. Laminated steel kitchen knife showing thin, exposed edge of high-carbon steel.

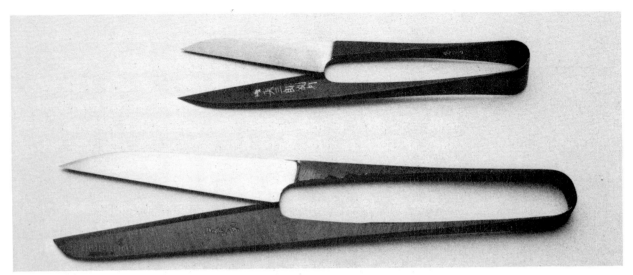

Fig. 193. Shears formed from a single strip of steel.

For pruning trees and shrubs, the Japanese pruning saws are unsurpassed. Their ¼ inch (6.3 mm)-long teeth with the secondary cutting bevel produce a very clean cut. With virtually no set to the teeth and a taper ground blade, they also cut very rapidly. They are found in both hardwood (seasoned) and softwood (green) tooth patterns. The most common blade length is about 8 inches (20.3 cm) and is available in two forms: a fixed blade presented in a wooden scabbard with belt loop, and a folding blade in which the blade rotates into the handle to protect the teeth when not in use.

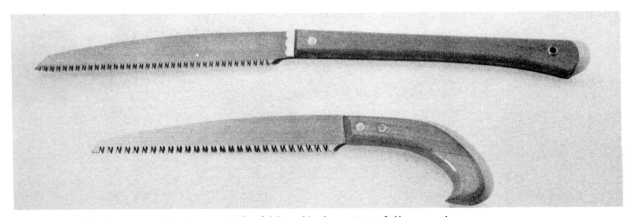

Fig. 194. Pruning saws: At the top is the folding-blade version, fully opened. At the bottom is the fixed-blade version.

Appendices

Appendix A

GLOSSARY

Annealing Heating and then cooling for the purpose of removing stresses or to induce softness.

Capillary Attraction A force that is the resultant of surface tension in liquids that are in contact with solids.

Carbon Steel Steel whose hardness depends solely on its carbon content.

Carburizing Adding carbon by heating steel in contact with a material rich in carbon. When followed by quenching, it case hardens the steel. Carbon absorption can be reduced by coating with "mud" compounds or copper plating.

Decarburization Loss of carbon from the surface of steel during heating and forging processes.

Forging Shaping a piece of metal while it is still hot by forming it with a hammer (either hand or power) on a press.

Grit Number Grit number is determined by grading the abrasive grains into uniform particle sizes by sifting them through mesh screens. The grid is made from silk threads of uniform cross sections which are positioned very accurately. The resulting grit number represents the number of opening in the screen per linear inch. Thus a 180-grit screen would have a 180 x 180 cross threads per inch or 32,400 opening per square inch. This system cannot be used by 240 grit, and in the finest screens the thickness of the threads themselves cause inaccuracies. Grit sizes about 240 must be graded by a flotation process using a gaseous or liquid carrier for the particles being separated.

Hardening   Heating above the critical temperature and then quenching to increase hardness.

Kerf   The narrow slot cut by a saw.

Line of Light   A dull edge on a cutting tool when held under a light will reflect the light off the flat of the edge, producing a "line of light" along the dull edge. A keen cutting edge will not reflect light, as it has no apparent thickness.

Parallax   The apparent change in the position of an object resulting from the change in direction from which it is viewed. It is also the difference in position of an object as seen by each eye.

Quenching   Cooling rapidly by immersion in oil or water.

Rockwell Hardness   is tested by measuring the resistance of the metal to a localized penetration. A Rockwell "C" hardness (R_C) is obtained by using a diamond with a conical point and a load of 150 kg (68 lbs) and reading the resulting number on a dial scale. For thin sections such as a saw blade, a finer loading system such as the micro-Vickers must be used.

Steel   The steel used in most chisel blades made in Japan is furnished by Hitachi. For better quality blades, the cutting edge is either "White Paper" high-carbon steel or "Blue Paper" alloy steel, and the soft body a low-carbon steel. For the chemical analysis of these steels, refer to the following chart. Since the carbon content of both "Blue Paper" and "White Paper" is identical, both steels can be heat treated to the same hardness level but the hardened "Blue Paper" steel will be somewhat tougher due to the alloy additives.

Materials for Japanese Chisels

	CARBON	SILICON	MANGANESE	PHOSPHORUS	SULFUR	CHROME	TUNGSTEN
	C %	Si %	Mn %	P %	S %	Cr %	W %
White Paper	1.0–1.2	0.10–0.20	0.20–0.30	0.025	0.004	—	—
Blue Paper	1.0–1.2	0.10–0.20	0.20–0.30	0.025	0.004	0.20–0.50	1.00–1.50

	C %	Si %	Mn %	P %	S %
Soft Steel	0.06	0.20	0.20	0.05	0.05

Swarf Residue from sharpening consisting of small chips of metal from the tool being sharpened and particles of worn abrasive grains.

Tempering Reheating after hardening to a temperature below the critical temperature, and then cooling.

Wrought Iron is made by burning off the carbon from molten iron and then hammering and rolling. The resulting material is very soft and ductile and easy to forge. When acid etched, it has a fibrous appearance similar to the grain structure of hickory. It can mistakenly be assumed to be a multi-laminate construction instead of a formation of slag inclusion which has been rolled out into long filaments. In well-made wrought iron there may be 200,000 slag fibres in an inch cross section.

Appendix B

BIBLIOGRAPHY

Sources Used by the Author

————. *A Hundred Pictures of Daiku at Work.* Japan: Shinkenchiku-sha Co. Ltd., 1974.

Faires, Virgil M. *Design of Machine Elements.* New York: Macmillan Publishing Co., 1965.

Iyoroi, ————. *Everything About Chisels.* Japan: Miki Chisel Association.

Ōdate, Toshio. *Japanese Woodworking Tools: Their Tradition, Spirit & Use.* Newtown, Connecticut: The Taunton Press, Inc., 1984.

Republic Steel Corporation. "Heat Treatment of Steels." 1961.

Salaman, R. S. *Dictionary of Tools Used in the Woodworking & Allied Trades c. 1700–1970.* New York: Scribner Publishing Co., 1976.

Uozumi, ————. *Production Process for Plane Blades.* Privately published monograph, 1984.

Story, Astona. *Wrought Iron, Its Manufacture, Characteristics & Application.* Am Byers Co., 1939.

Yoshida, Yoshio. *Collection of Carpenter's Tools.* Japan: Shinkenchiku-Co., Ltd., 1985.

Recommended Reading Material

For the woodworker who wants to learn more about the techniques of Japanese joinery or details on Japanese house framing, I can recommend the following books:

Engel, Heinrich. *Measurement and Construction of the Japanese House*. C. E. Tuttle Publishing Co., 1985.

Nakuhara, Yasuo. *Japanese Joinery: A Handbook for Joiners & Carpenters*. Hartley & Marks Publishing Co.

Seike, Kiyosi. *Art of Japanese Joinery*. Weatherhill Publishing Co.

For details on the construction of *shoji,* the paper-covered sliding screens that are the hallmark of the Japanese house, see the article "Japanese Sliding Doors" by Toshio Ōdate in *Fine Woodworking* magazine (volume 34). Copies of the above books are available from most of the catalog sources listed in Appendix D. However, at this time Garrett Wade Company is the only mail order source to stock the translucent papers used in making *shoji.*

Appendix C

ENGLISH/JAPANESE EQUIVALENT TERMS

Tools

English Terms	Japanese Terms
Adze	Chōna
Axe	Ono
Chisel	Nomi
Butt Chisel	Oire-nomi
Thick Chisel	At su-homi
Clamp	Hatagane
Hammer (general)	Tsuchi
Hammer (carpenter's)	Gennō
Marking (cutting) gauge	Keshiki
Plane	Kanna
Saw	Nokogiri
Backsaw	Dōzuki (literally "tenon shoulder")
Crosscut/rip combination (two-sided saw)	Ryoba
Single edge rip or crosscut saw	Kataba
Sharpening stones	Toishi

Woods

English Terms	Japanese Terms
Boxwood	Gumi
Cedar	Sugi
Chestnut	Kuri

Cypress	Hinoki
Mulberry	Kuwa
Poplar	Hō
Red Oak	Akagashi
White Oak	Gashi
Paulownia	Kiri
Zelkova (mountain ash)	Keyaki

METRIC CHART

MM—MILLIMETRES   CM—CENTIMETRES

INCHES TO MILLIMETRES AND CENTIMETRES

INCHES	MM	CM	INCHES	CM	INCHES	CM
⅛	3	0.3	9	22.9	30	76.2
¼	6	0.6	10	25.4	31	78.7
⅜	10	1.0	11	27.9	32	81.3
½	13	1.3	12	30.5	33	83.8
⅝	16	1.6	13	33.0	34	86.4
¾	19	1.9	14	35.6	35	88.9
⅞	22	2.2	15	38.1	36	91.4
1	25	2.5	16	40.6	37	94.0
1¼	32	3.2	17	43.2	38	96.5
1½	38	3.8	18	45.7	39	99.1
1¾	44	4.4	19	48.3	40	101.6
2	51	5.1	20	50.8	41	104.1
2½	64	6.4	21	53.3	42	106.7
3	76	7.6	22	55.9	43	109.2
3½	89	8.9	23	58.4	44	111.8
4	102	10.2	24	61.0	45	114.3
4½	114	11.4	25	63.5	46	116.8
5	127	12.7	26	66.0	47	119.4
6	152	15.2	27	68.6	48	121.9
7	178	17.8	28	71.1	49	124.5
8	203	20.3	29	73.7	50	127.0

Japanese units of length

1 shaku = 10 sun = 100 bu = 11.93 inches
1 bu = 0.12 inches = 3.03 mm

1 foot = 1.01 shaku = 305 mm
1 inch = 8.38 bu = 25.4 mm

Index